interface design

ALISTAIR DABBS

SERIES CONSULTANT
ALASTAIR CAMPBELL

WATSON-GUPTILL
PUBLICATIONS
New York

First published in the United States in 2002 by Watson-Guptill Publications, a division of VNU Business Media, Inc., 770 Broadway, New York, NY 10003

This book was conceived, designed and produced by The Ilex Press Ltd The Barn College Farm 1 West End Whittlesford Cambridge CB2 4LX

Sales Office The Old Candlemakers West Street, Lewes East Sussex BN7 2NZ

Publisher:
Sophie Collins
Art Director:
Alastair Campbell
Editorial Director:
Steve Luck
Design Manager:
Tony Seddon
Project Editor:
Rowan Davies
Designers:
Jane and Chris Lanaway

www.designdirectories.com

Originated and printed by Hong Kong Graphics and Printing Ltd, China

Library of Congress Cataloging-in-Publication Data
Dabbs, Alistair
    Interface design / Alistair Dabbs
        p. cm.
    ISBN 0-8230-2516-0
        1. Computer software—Development.
        2. Human–computer interaction.
        I. Title
    QA76.76.D47 D33
    2002
    005.1—dc21
        2001 007639

CONTENTS

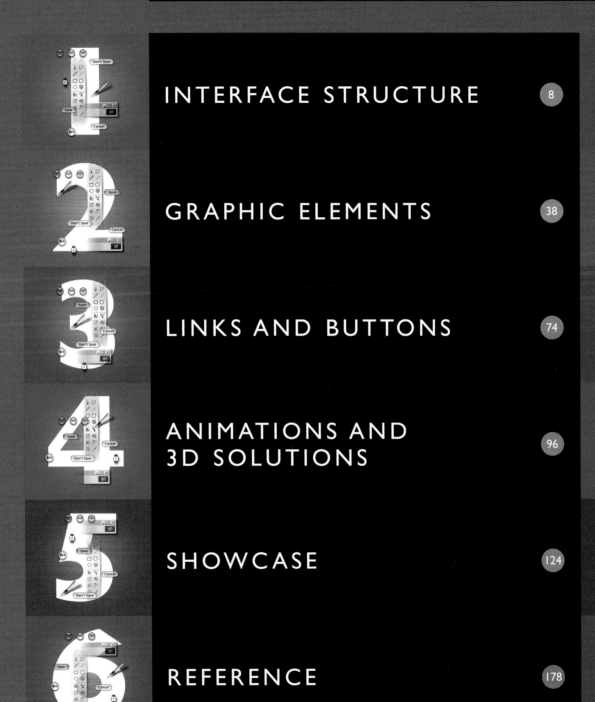

INTERFACE STRUCTURE — 8

GRAPHIC ELEMENTS — 38

LINKS AND BUTTONS — 74

ANIMATIONS AND
3D SOLUTIONS — 96

SHOWCASE — 124

REFERENCE — 178

WINDOW ON THE DIGITAL WORLD

The term "interface" has various differing meanings within the extensive field of modern computers. For a hardware engineer, it is used to refer to the plug-and-socket arrangements that are set up between machines. For a system integrator, it is used to refer to the data-cabling standard. However, for the graphic designer (and software programmer, too), it's the stuff that you see on a computer screen. These elements—on-screen text, graphics, windows, icons, and so on—are the things that we'll investigate in depth throughout this book.

The dictionary definition of an interface is "a common point or boundary between two things." Thus, it follows that the digital interface is the medium that is placed between humans and binary data. With the computerization of everything at the beginning of the 21st century—from business information and newspapers to entertainment and household devices—the interfaces on various devices are our best chance of acquiring a good understanding of it all. However, as every microwave oven owner knows, something that seems like a good interface to the product designers doesn't necessarily work in "real life."

Just as people complain about programming their video cassette recorders at home, or become bemused by the complexity of the half-load wool economy setting on their washing machines, on-screen interfaces to computers seem to engender just as much frustration as praise. This can occur in many different settings: at sites on the Web, in multimedia presentations, on mobile phones, in shopping mall booths, and in the newly emerging field of interactive video. *Interface Design* investigates why certain approaches simply don't work, reveals common errors, and provides essential advice on how to do it right.

The book starts with the fundamentals of interfaces, explaining the delimiting factors of a digital system—such as software design and operating systems as well as

The Web site for the Guiness Storehouse in Dublin presents an innovative virtual "tour" of its museum using Flash technology.

2
The concept of "skins"—in which many different graphic interfaces exist for the same technology—allows the user an important element of personal choice.

3
Another innovative piece of interface design: the industrial design studio Ideo presents its portfolio as a wide, horizontally scrolling page of thumbnails.

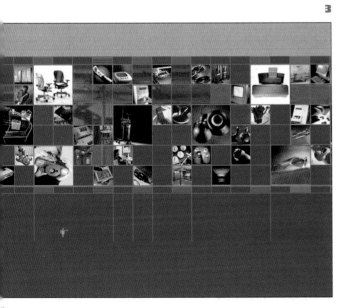

3

the commonly adopted concepts of scrolling, navigating, and interactivity. It then takes a more in-depth look at the graphic elements that make up interfaces and examines the role and potential of color, typography, and other visual clues. This is followed by practical, nitty-gritty advice about the key issue of navigation in any interface. It's more than just having "forward" and "back" arrows: there are links, triggers, and integration with other sources of information that must also be sorted out. Even if people know where you want them to go, is it where they want to go? Do they know where they are? Or how to get out?

The next chapter brings you bang up-to-date with the world of interactive computer animation and 3D graphics. It covers the latest programs and solutions in order to teach you about the construction and practical uses of Web movies, virtual meeting spaces, dynamic panoramas, and educational walk throughs.

Finally, *Interface Design* concludes with an extensive showcase of digital interfaces that have been designed by the most imaginative minds around. Thought provoking and often surprising, these samples of Web sites, programs, navigational aids, presentations, and electrical devices should inspire you to take your own designs to the next level.

The Web explosion that has occurred over the last ten years has opened up the potential for just about everyone to present themselves and their companies or organizations to the world. Inevitably, most people who pick up this book will have some interest in Web design, or at least Web-distributed design, so rest assured you'll find plenty of working material on that subject along with everything else.

In showing you how to look beyond the predictable and pedestrian, this book will force you to rethink your approach to design in the digital age to make the most of its true, unrestricted potential.

INTRODUCING THE DIGITAL INTERFACE 10

MULTIPLE PLATFORMS 12

THE GUI IN MODERN OPERATING SYSTEMS 16

CURSORS AND ICONS 18

DIALOGUE WINDOWS AND MESSAGES 20

TOOL AND RIBBON BARS 22

FLOATING PALETTES 24

CONCEPTS OF SCROLLING 26

PROGRESSIVE PAGING 28

BUILDING SLIDE SHOWS 30

ADDING MULTIMEDIA 32

INTERACTIVITY 34

THE WEB EXPLOSION 36

8

INTRODUCING THE DIGITAL INTERFACE

The computing revolution of the past 25 years has brought about massive changes in the way we live. Processing power, miniaturization, and the way in which computers interact with people have all improved.

In the 1940s and 1950s, computers were operated by turning cogs and throwing switches, and people had to know a good deal about what lay underneath before they knew what to turn or flick on the front. Every computing task involved programming in those days. By the 1960s and 1970s, programs and data were stored on magnetic tape and later disks, and corporate data-processing tasks could be controlled with dextrous manipulation of punched cards. Only when someone came up with the idea of attaching a cathode ray tube to a computer and letting operators communicate with the machine using a typewriter keyboard was the truly digital interface born.

3 | 4 | 5

It's a Windows world according to Microsoft, but if you look at what the company had to offer in its earlier operating systems in terms of interface design, you will find perplexing stuff indeed. DOS programs (3) did the best they could to give an attractive style to what was purely a text-based interface. Things improved by the release of Windows 3.x (4) at the end of the 1980s, made rapid interface gains through the 1990s, and culminated in the soft look of Windows XP (5).

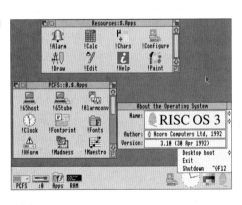

1 | 2

The current leaders of the personal computing business might be Apple Macintosh and the Windows-based PC, but don't forget there have been other systems that presented challenges. To this day, many people still swear by the powerful and graphically rich Acorn Archimedes (1) and Atari (2) platforms.

10

Today's interfaces are barely recognizable from those developed in the early days. However, you don't have to look back too far to discover that the development of good digital interfaces has been a painful experience, and we're not finished with it yet. Over the years, especially since the concept of the "graphical user interface," or GUI, many assumptions have been made about what is good and what is bad in on-screen digital design. These have been built upon, and built upon further, until the builders forget why they made the assumption in the first place.

Take a look backward before charging ahead with your own ideas about what makes a good interface; try to challenge the assumptions of the digital generation. Who says that drop-down menus are the best approach? Why should Web pages scroll vertically and not horizontally? And perhaps you should ask yourself why, even after 25 years, novices still find computers—and now also mobile phones, video players, and game consoles—so hard to come to grips with.

6 | 7 | 8
Personal computing actually began with machines like Apple's Lisa, whose interface (6) was said to have been based on ideas from Xerox in the late 1970s. Many of today's assumptions about digital interfaces were originally laid down here, such as drop-down menus, windows, and title bars. Indeed, the operating system for the Apple Macintosh (8) right up until 2001 differed only in the detail, not the core design. Mac OS X (7) maintains some of these concepts, but signifies a new animated direction for computer interfaces.

MULTIPLE PLATFORMS

Paging through this book, you'll find many examples of software interfaces as they appear on what is commonly referred to as "mainstream personal computers": Macs and PCs. As a designer, you must be aware that the impact of digital interfaces goes way beyond this narrow outlook as everything with a screen needs an interface.

Look around you and see the variety of electronic devices out there: not just desktop computers but notebook, handheld, and palmtop computers too. As screen size decreases, the interface needs to be better in order to make the most of the available size. The issue of size throws out a whole bunch of questions that need to be answered. Lacking the luxury of screen space, how do you deal with long menus? How do you squeeze in big pictures and long text documents? Do you have enough room for on-screen buttons?

These are all issues for product designers and programmers, and you may not be involved in this kind of work. But people may well be using these same devices to access something that you have created independently, so start asking yourself more questions. Can your Microsoft PowerPoint presentation be viewed on a business handheld computer? What will your button-crazy Web pages look like on a black-and-white palmtop? Have you created a Flash-only site that will therefore be rendered unreadable by all but the most expensive machines?

Your interface also needs to take into account the way that different devices are operated. Some have buttons, others use styluses; some can even be spoken to. Maybe you're designing something to be shown on a boardroom projector or video wall, where user control is remote and awkward. Or perhaps it's a point-of-sale booth where there's no keyboard or mouse, and everything must be manipulated by touch. Will people with big fingers have trouble with your small buttons? How long will it take them to type in their address, and will they give up before finishing?

1 | 2

Palmtop computers enjoy plenty of software programs created specifically for them. For example, Microsoft Reader (1) for the PocketPC platform lets users read ebooks in a small format that suits the screen. Designers can optimize ebooks during their creation to take advantage of this. But palmtops need to stay in touch with the outside world too. Look at how Internet Explorer (2) under PocketPC deals with Web sites by using a zoom-out function, which isn't always successful. What will your Web site look like on a palmtop screen such as this?

3

3

Sub-notebooks and some of the larger handheld computers, such as this Psion Series 7, keep the screen clear by putting permanent icon buttons alongside the screen. There may also be certain customary interface design expectations for particular platforms, such as a second row of on-screen buttons like the blue ones shown here.

5

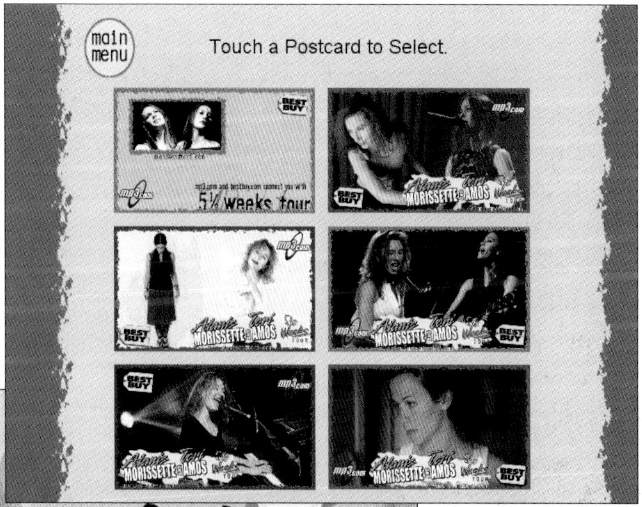

13

4 | 5

Here are two screens from customer point-of-sale booths. Notice how big the buttons are, and that they include full images instead of just thumbnails or icons. One interface is clearly designed to work with a keyboard —and a swipe card.

4

MULTIPLE PLATFORMS II

If you think palmtop computers have small screens, think again. The most widespread computing platform in the Western world is the mobile phone, and its screen is positively tiny. But even though it is tiny, you still have options from a creative point of view. There may only be enough room for a few short lines of text, but it's up to you to present the text in a useful and readable way. Even laser printers and washing machines with one-line liquid crystal display (LCD) windows have to have their interfaces designed to some degree.

The mobile phone is a particular challenge simply because it's so common, and because it is increasingly becoming an Internet-enabled device. Once a mobile-phone user tries to access your Web site—compacted down as a WAP (wireless application protocol) site—you take almost complete control over the phone interface. This is worth bearing in mind, especially if you also listen to the stories of WAP woe. Only half the problems with WAP concern compatibility and reliability issues; the other half can be attributed to incomprehensible menus and prompts.

14

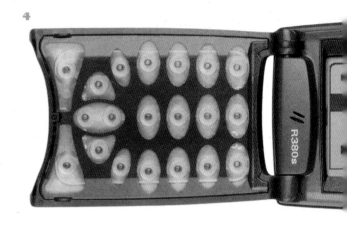

4

1 | 2 | 3
Mobile phones can only support basic graphics, but designers can use this for branding, or to make the site identity very clear. If the user can recognize your site icon at arm's length, you're doing

well. This must then be cleared away and replaced with text. Designers should ensure that the text has sensible list lengths, logical navigation, and mini-branding at the top of the screen.

4
Here's one way to enlarge the screen on a mobile phone without significantly increasing the size of the phone itself. The interface uses a tab analogy and big icons for touch-screen navigation.

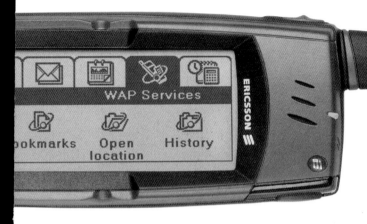

5

...ample
...of mobile
...hould be
...hin the
...rs. Note
...lor

...future
...gn, which
...npact on
...ign, too,
...l in the
...ction

...24–177).

7

When WAP became a mainstream application, there was one particularly beneficial side effect: phone manufacturers finally became prepared to be persuaded to make the phone screens a little more generous in size. This had the effect of making the entire phone interface more suitable for such functions as scrolling through address books, calendars, and SMS (short message service) messages. As time goes on, and greater and greater numbers of personal information management functions are being built into business phones, the screens are getting even bigger, and some are also being converted to color. At the same time, palmtops are becoming more similar to mobile phones. Therefore you should confidently expect to be designing for these platforms more often in the future.

THE GUI IN MODERN OPERATING SYSTEMS

It is important to challenge any assumptions that you come up against, but you shouldn't reject everything in the form in which it exists at the moment. For better or worse, computer interfaces have grown up in an organic way since the original ideas were first borne out of technical minds. But even these minds were borrowing ideas from other people who had come before them. Whoever first said, "Let's have data put into 'files,' and put these files into 'folders,'" was obviously trying to copy what was seen as a familiar concept to office workers. Such workers dealt with bits of paper that they kept in mobile folders, which in turn went into filing cabinets. Logical enough, right?

Well, what if you're not an office worker? What if you're an athlete? Or a bus driver? Or an alcoholic? If the originators of the common GUI had thought about this rather than simply considering their beloved offices, today's operating system interface might involve filling on-screen bottles with data booze and locking them away in a liquor cabinet.

The problem is that now that we have gone so far with the original concepts, it's hard to go back and totally re-invent the founding concepts of interface design, as it is very doubtful that they'd catch on. Even if your interface doesn't deal with document files and folders, it must recognize that these concepts exist in the background. Ignoring them, altering their accepted hierarchical structure, or even changing what they're called would just cause confusion.

Having such basics already laid down for you can actually often be helpful. Since computer users generally understand the ground rules of files, folders, and windows, you can use them within your interface without having to explain them. Show the user two windows and a file icon, and they'll know they can drag the file from one window to the other. These ground rules can make your interface cleaner.

16

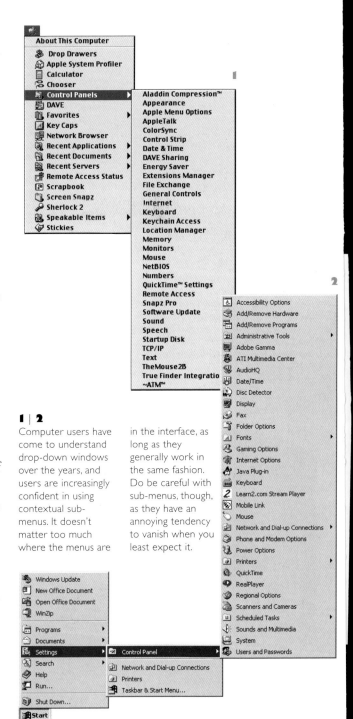

1 | 2

Computer users have come to understand drop-down windows over the years, and users are increasingly confident in using contextual sub-menus. It doesn't matter too much where the menus are in the interface, as long as they generally work in the same fashion. Do be careful with sub-menus, though, as they have an annoying tendency to vanish when you least expect it.

3 | 4

Modern operating systems do more than show file and folder icons—they also let the user drill down into the folder structure to find documents that are buried several layers down. If you have to provide some kind of archival search option for those viewing the presentation, don't feel that you have to restrict the interface to big, clumsy windows.

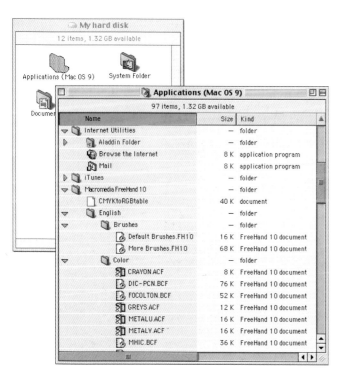

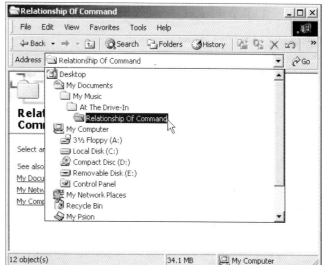

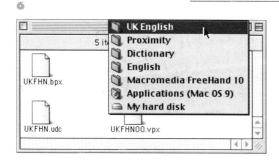

5 | 6

The method by which users can extract themselves from a deep folder after drilling down into it is not so standardized. This means that you can't rely upon a user's knowledge to "get back out," so you'll have to show how to do it explicitly in your interface. We'll cover navigation in depth in "Links and Buttons" (see pages 74–95).

CURSORS AND ICONS

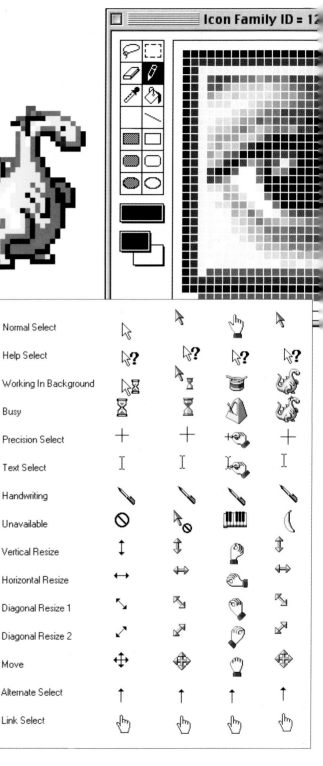

Just as with the previously-discussed examples of files and folders, computer users gradually have grown accustomed to the way a mouse pointer, or "cursor," looks and feels in all the available mainstream operating systems. This means that when you present something that is different from what is widely anticipated by the public, you are effectively raising another obstacle for your viewers to overcome. So don't make the pointer arrow face to the right or make it bright red—at least not without a clear reason.

Certain software environments will let you customize cursors fully; Java applets and Macromedia ShockWave movies are two examples. It can be fun to enliven the look of custom interfaces with custom cursors, but it will only be appreciated if people can recognize what they're supposed to be. When the viewer clicks, will the result be an expected one? If the cursor is pictorial, does it conform to what the picture represents in the viewer's mind? A classic example of one that doesn't work exactly as expected is the Paintbrush cursor found in so many graphics packages and in plenty of interactive multimedia titles, too. Often, a defined area in a picture is filled with color by clicking in it with a Paintbrush cursor. But paint brushes in real life are brushed—that is, people expect to use them with a brushing motion, not by just planting them in one place. And in real life, you absorb paint into the brush by dipping the brush into the paint can—whoever heard of using an eyedropper to do this? Much the same goes for icons, which are pictorial representations given to programs, files, folders, storage volumes, hardware devices, (printers, scanners, etc.) and virtual locations. When designing icons, think about what kind of impression they'll make on someone who sees them for the first time. An icon should tell the viewer what kind of object it is, not just its theme.

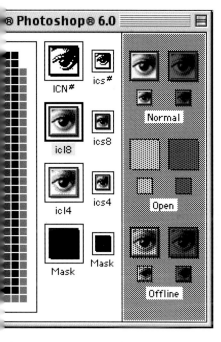

3

Don't assume that animating an icon is a shallow gimmick and a waste of resources, as it can fulfill a useful role. When downloading a file from the Internet using Microsoft Internet Explorer for the Mac, for example, the animated file icon updates to indicate the progress of the download transfer.

So a multimedia aquarium program could have an icon that looks like a fish. But if you make other files look like types of fish, such as "Read Me" documents and how-to guides, the viewer won't know what's what. Yes, it's clichéd, but if text document icons look like pieces of paper and picture file icons look like little *Mona Lisa*s, you're giving everyone a chance to immediately understand what they're seeing, rather than making them guess. After all, if you leave things to chance, they may guess wrong and your interface quickly fails as a result. An icon is supposed to be a visual aid, not a hindrance.

 19

1

Even basic mouse cursors for navigating an operating system will change according to the context they are used in. Here's the standard set that is included with Windows, along with some brighter and animated alternatives: 3D Bronze, Conductor, and Dinosaur.

2

Creating and editing good icons is something of a fine art. You can design them from scratch using pixel-by-pixel tools, as shown here, or start off with a larger image and shrink it down afterward.

4

While program icons can be designed to look like just about anything, it's important that files and hardware objects are given icons that are easily recognizable as to what they represent. From this collection, can you work out which icons are for picture, movie, audio, and font files? And which are folders, text documents, business charts, and slide presentations? Can you instantly pick out the ones that point to floppy disks, CD-ROMs, printers, and stuff that needs to be deleted?

 4

DIALOGUE WINDOWS AND MESSAGES

Designers do not always consider the basics of program interfaces to be their job. "That's something for programmers," many say. Yet something as simple as a dialogue window that prompts a user for an ID and password needs designing, even if it's going to be gray with a plain title bar. Think about how big the window should be. Where should the OK and Cancel buttons go? Is the text clear enough, and will it still be clear if the user has changed the default font for the operating

20

3

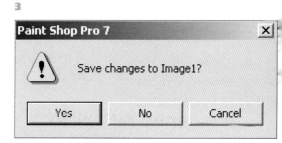

1

From a theoretical point of view, there's nothing wrong with this form. It has been made to align flush on the left and right of the dialogue window.

3

If you try to close an image or exit the program without saving, Paint Shop Pro asks what you want to do with the unsaved picture: "Yes" to save and close, "No" to close without saving, and "Cancel" to neither save nor close (i.e., to continue editing the picture).

2

From a design point of view, this is better. The form fields (the most striking visual aspect) have been lined up, and the labels are ragged.

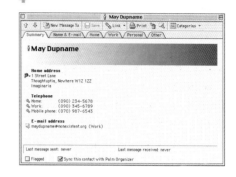

system? These issues crop up in all kinds of interface work. Computer games, distributable presentations, and program installers all prompt users for information and send error messages and confirmations occasionally.

The first golden rule is consistency, consistency, consistency. Even if the interface is uninspiring, at least you can make it predictable and unchallenging to use. If someone has to keep saying, "Now what do I do here?" then there's obviously a problem. This leads onto the second golden rule: don't hide functionality simply to keep the interface Zen. While too many toggles and pop-up menus can be confusing, you shouldn't ever force users to hunt for clues.

Finally, pity the poor person filling out a form. Have you ever tried filling out an application form, tax form, or e-commerce order form on-line yourself? When you got something wrong or forgot to complete one of the fields, what kind of error message was thrown back in your face? Think about these frustrating experiences when it's your turn to design a form.

Electronic forms often work best split over progressive screens rather than presented as one huge document. Topics need to be grouped logically. Fields look "right" when aligned: if some fields are mandatory and others are not, make them clearly distinguishable.

4
By incorporating tab views in a dialogue window, you can cram lots of options in without forcing the viewer to open several windows.

Microsoft Entourage gives each tab in its Address Book a familiar name, as well as providing a summary tab at the front.

5
QuarkXPress combines four context-sensitive dialogue windows into one overall Modify dialogue. Four different keyboard shortcuts allow you to open the window with the desired tab selected and brought to the front.

21

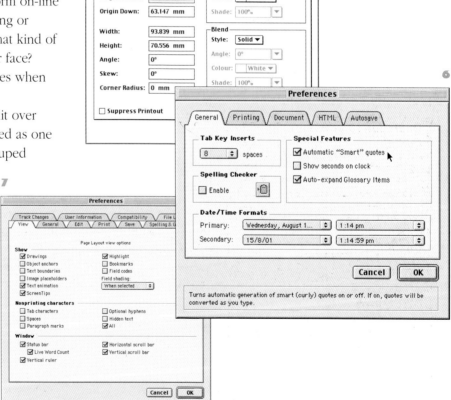

6
Z-Write's tabbed Preferences window includes a two-line panel at the bottom that provides extra help or an expanded explanation of each option as you move the mouse pointer around.

7
Now things get complicated. Microsoft Word's Preferences window introduces two rows of tabs. The active row then leaps to the front and you've immediately lost the way back.

TOOL AND RIBBON BARS

If the original GUI revolution introduced drop-down menus, windows, and icons to the world, there must have been a second revolution somewhere along the way that added ribbon bars, tool bars, and floating palettes to the mix. Palettes are dealt with separately (*see page 24*) because they are largely a programming design concept. Button bars, on the other hand, have crossed over into general-purpose interface design in much the same way as custom icons.

A ribbon bar is a row of buttons that carry out a specific function when clicked. Microsoft has pretty much standardized the look and feel of ribbon bars in mainstream operating systems through the influential interface design of its Office software suite. The result is that you may well be forced to follow the leader here if your own digital interface makes use of a row of on-screen buttons. Microsoft's concepts for common computer functions, such as File Open, File Save, File New, Copy, Paste, and so on, may not be ideal, but millions of people are already familiar with them.

Of course, the nature of your digital presentation may not cover the usual, well-known program functions, in which case you can let your imagination run wild. Just remember that on-screen buttons in ribbon bars were first invented to serve two needs. One was to put regularly used commands up front in the interface, to save the user from having to wade through drop-down menus. The other was to do it graphically in a tiny amount of screen space instead of presenting the commands as a worded list, as you often find in 3D and CAD (computer-aided design) packages. So if your

22

1
The principle behind ribbon bars is to make commonly used commands instantly available rather than hiding them under the menus. But you can go too far. Remember, there's a reason why commands are hidden in the menus: it saves screen space.

2
One way of reducing screen clutter is to let viewers customize the interface. Here, a pop-up menu in Word's main ribbon bar allows various buttons to be displayed or hidden as preferred. Then again, there's something slightly curious about designing a ribbon bar so that you don't need to navigate menus and then promptly putting a menu in it.

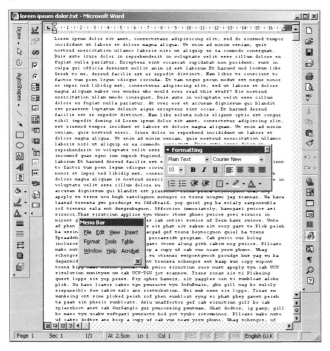

buttons are not self-explanatory, are too big, or pop up their own mini menus, then you've missed the point and your viewer will soon lose the plot.

A tool bar is a row (or alternatively, and more commonly, a column) of buttons. When used individually, the buttons will send the active program into a particular editing mode. Because of this, tool bars do not occur frequently as elements of everyday interface design; they are more likely to be pressed into use in application programming. But because tool bars are so familiar to computer users due to graphics software and even modern word processors, you can borrow some of their concepts for your own design work. Tools and cursors must run consistently, however—*see page 18* for more tips on the latter.

23

4

5

6

7

3

When your interface fills the screen or needs to be completely self-contained within a program window, you might consider letting viewers choose where the ribbons and tools

should go. For example, perhaps they don't like the traditional location at the top, but would rather the ribbons ran down the sides or along the bottom, or would want them to float as palettes.

4 | 5 | 6 | 7

Like it or lump it, there is a generally acknowledged interface "standard" for ribbon bars that the computing industry associates with Microsoft Office software. To match the look of the Office

ribbon bar, the buttons need to be of a similar size and general appearance, even if the bulk of the buttons themselves are going to be different from one program to the next. Here you can see

Microsoft Word (4), Paint Shop Pro (5), Corel Photo-Paint (6), and Macromedia FreeHand (7). Even FreeHand, which avoids direct copying of the Office button graphics, follows the Office ribbon format.

FLOATING PALETTES

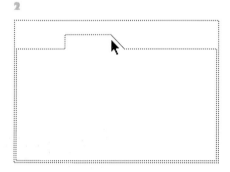

1

1 Although tabbed palettes are supposed to save screen space, constantly clicking between them will drive a viewer nuts. So let them be separated. For example, if you click on a tab in Adobe Illustrator…

24

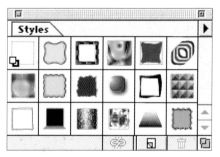

2
… and drag it to one side, away from the original palette …

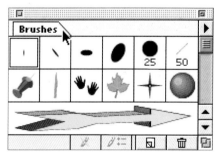

3 | 4
… it separates the two tabs into two independently floating windows. You can always drag them back together later on if necessary.

Also known as a "panel," "tool window," and "floating dialogue," the floating palette is an interface element that has grown in importance in recent years. The idea behind it was to provide the software user with a little window containing all the key functions of a particular editing mode, or perhaps a group of commands that share the same theme. This is actually the same concept that was behind the dialogue window *(see page 20),* but in a palette it is presented in a more compact manner and is kept on-screen at all times: that is, it doesn't need to be dismissed by clicking an OK or Cancel button. The fundamental difference between dialogue windows and floating palettes from a programmer's point of view is the processing power. Older generation computers had to be given commands through menus and dialogues, and then also had to be told to go ahead and carry them out. Modern computers, however, are powerful enough to maintain up-to-date on-screen information in "real time" as the same kinds of changes are made.

Floating palettes aren't found in all software packages, so the concept isn't as familiar as standard dialogue windows are. And, of course, the opportunity to create floating palettes is much more restricted outside of software design. However, an understanding of what floating palettes are supposed to offer will actually help all your interface work, especially when you are using tool bars and dialogues.

Above all other issues, a floating palette needs to be concise and tightly compact. Remember that it's going to be hanging around on-screen all the time, occupying space. See here how various software design teams have attempted to meet this challenge by using collapsing title bars, docking areas, and tabs.

5

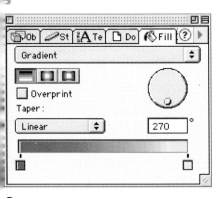

5
Often, palette tabs are too small to be read, so it pays to employ mini-icon indicators alongside the text, as is done in Macromedia FreeHand.

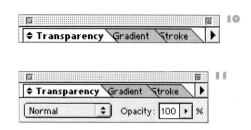
10

11

6
Another handy idea is to allow your palettes to be expanded just like a program window by dragging on a corner or edge. This can then allow tab headings to expand fully, even if the palette tools themselves don't need the space.

6

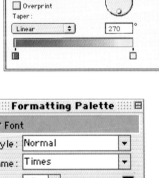

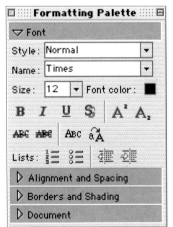

12

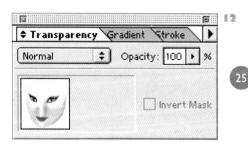

25

13

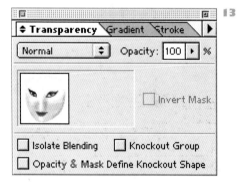

7 | 8 | 9
Yet another approach to floating and expanding palettes is demonstrated here by Microsoft Word (7) for Mac's Formatting Palette (8). The base palette is tiny, but it expands section by section as required.

10 | 11 | 12 | 13
There's more than one way to save screen space with floating palettes, but without minimizing or dismissing them altogether. Tiny up-down arrows shown in any tab in Adobe Illustrator indicate that the palette can be shrunk or expanded progressively with a sequence of clicks.

8

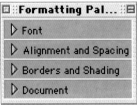

7

9

CONCEPTS OF SCROLLING

When a page won't fit onto the screen, you can usually get to it by "scrolling." This involves pushing bits of a document off the screen so that you get to see the bits that were previously hidden. Scrolling has become a way of life for computer users: it is incorporated in just about everything.

Because scrolling is so common, it's easy to forget that it's as much an obstacle as a handy device. Certain kinds of interface must not scroll, because doing so would be unexpected and impractical. Examples of these include point-of-sale booths, entry-level educational titles, and big-screen presentations. When divorced from their own convenient desktops and accurate mice, computer users will stumble around unfamiliar interfaces clumsily. If the interface is built around a booth trackball or touchscreen, don't force users to drag on scroll bars. They'll just give up.

You should not expect an audience to understand what's happening if you start scrolling during a presentation. It is better to avoid it altogether. Scrolling makes viewers forget where they started, especially when the interface is unfamiliar. Putting a message on-screen that says "Scroll down for more information" will often fail to register with the viewer, as their eyes are darting around the screen looking for content that's there rather than instructions on content that you've hidden. An interface should never be a treasure hunt.

Anyone working in Web design should be aware of this issue. People tend only to scroll Web pages when they know that there's something worth looking for. With e-commerce sites, booths, or on-screen catalogues, don't expect anyone to look beyond the top of the page.

If you thought vertical scrolling was challenging, unintentional horizontal scroll bars are the official seal of failure on a design. You can be creative with horizontal scrolling if you're confident about the viewer's ability, but in general people find it irritating beyond measure.

1
Many content-heavy Web sites require viewers to scroll down the page. In case they don't bother, all the most important content is crammed into the top of the page.

2
Here's what you couldn't see in the initial window. Excite's intention is to present a busy page, but many casual viewers may never get to see any of it; be wary of this pitfall.

3

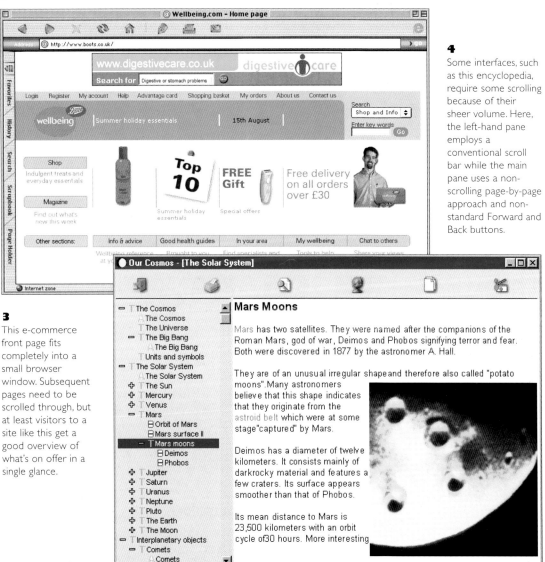

4

Some interfaces, such as this encyclopedia, require some scrolling because of their sheer volume. Here, the left-hand pane employs a conventional scroll bar while the main pane uses a non-scrolling page-by-page approach and non-standard Forward and Back buttons.

5 | 6 | 7 | 8

Small screens force scrolling—you have no choice about that. So take a tip from WAP site designers, who are required to work with the smallest screens of all—mobile phones. Content needs to be presented with the most popular items at the top of each list. The lists themselves should be short, and even your choice of headings, link names, and running text itself needs to employ short words. Note also the permanent availability of the Back button and a link to Options. Many of these techniques from a Zen design environment like WAP can be applied to other small-window interfaces where scrolling is inevitable.

27

3

This e-commerce front page fits completely into a small browser window. Subsequent pages need to be scrolled through, but at least visitors to a site like this get a good overview of what's on offer in a single glance.

4

5

6

7

8

PROGRESSIVE PAGING

A sequence of screens in a presentation should be logical and natural from the viewer's perspective. This, in turn, mirrors the way in which people read printed documents page by page, and maintains an order by which viewers know whether they are going forward or backward in the presentation. However, this isn't how all people read in the real world. Some skip through bits, check something a few pages later, and then jump back; others read the ending first, and many put the book down to study other material before going back to it. Of course, reproducing such messy techniques in your interface would be a disaster, but you can take advantage of the on-screen medium to add value to the progressive paging model.

Think of your pages or screenfuls as being made up of layers, some visible and others waiting to materialize. A presentation software package illustrates this concept well. Although the presentation is a sequence of screens, each screen itself can be built up progressively. For example, the text might appear piece by piece, followed next by a graphic, then by annotations to that graphic and possibly an animation when a button is clicked on. There may also be links to other pages or to Web sites, and you may allow viewers to decide in what order these "layers" are added to the page. Yet it's still one self-contained page in the sequence you created originally. Your interface has lost nothing in its logical layout but has gained a great deal in functionality.

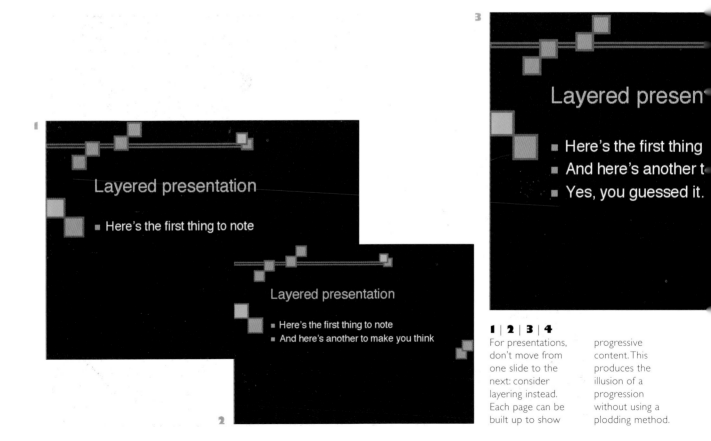

1 | 2 | 3 | 4
For presentations, don't move from one slide to the next: consider layering instead. Each page can be built up to show progressive content. This produces the illusion of a progression without using a plodding method.

As always, it remains vitally important to be consistent in your work. In order to present a progressive sequence that your audience will be able to follow, the pages need to share the same styling chracteristics; if you stray from consistency, then your audience will be frustrated and possibly lost. It is essential that you keep this in mind when you are layering the pages. You may also want to maintain a consistent style in the way in which the layering is applied: for example, the ways in which text slides onto the screen, colors change, animations are presented, which transition effects are employed, and other such matters. Take a tip from Web designers and keep to the same restricted set of fonts, colors, and layout across an entire site.

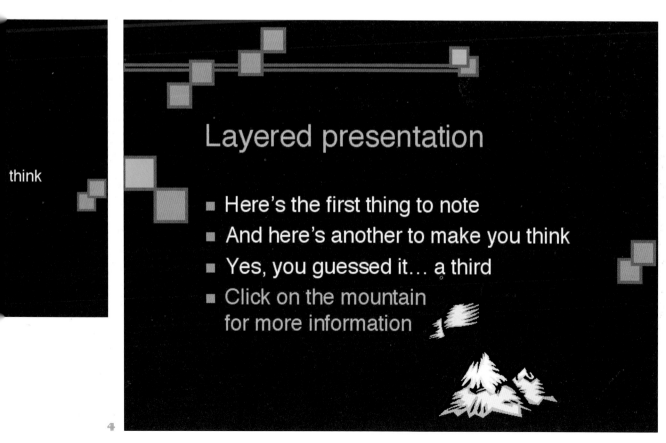

BUILDING SLIDE SHOWS

Let's face up to the fact that many presentation-style interfaces won't afford you the luxury of layering pages. And even if they do, would you really want them to? When you're in control of the presentation, you can pack as many triggers and animated effects into each page as you like. But when you put everything into the viewer's hands, you need to make it much simpler. A self-running or partly interactive presentation for people to run on their own computers must be extremely simple to use, unless you intend to distribute a user manual with the presentation.

This is where the old slide show approach comes in, because nothing is simpler than tapping a key on the keyboard or clicking a mouse button to progress a preset sequence of screens in the order they were originally intended. You could build in an automatic timer sequence to make the show entirely self-playing. But there are ways of making a slide show more usable and interactive than the concept first suggests. The most important thing to do is build in some simple navigation tools so that the viewer can skip forward or jump back easily. If the only way a viewer can get out of a sequence is to exit the entire presentation, then he or she will do just that and probably won't come back.

30

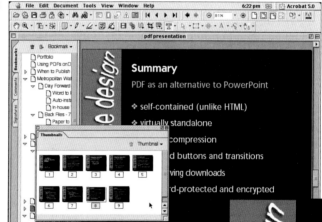

1

You might like to distribute slide shows in Acrobat PDF format. This way, anyone with the Acrobat Reader installed on his or her computer can immediately open, view, and print your presentation. However, useful features such as Bookmarks and Thumbnails can get in the way.

4

PowerPoint is found in millions of PCs and Macs, but you may not want to use it for distributing your presentations. Even if viewers have the program, they may not know how to use it. The presentation could even be edited and redistributed under false pretenses. Try exporting the slideshow to QuickTime movie format instead.

2

To avoid Bookmarks and Thumbnails, consider changing the Document Open Options so that the PDF opens in Full Screen Mode, while hiding the menu and tool bars.

3

The result will appear to run like a PowerPoint-style presentation at the full size and resolution of the viewer's monitor. Make sure that you include basic navigation buttons if you do this, of course.

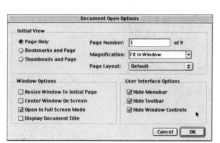

5 | 6

Although QuickTime versions of presentations tend to make large files, they can incorporate animation effects such as blended transitions. They can also be viewer-controlled (using the cursor keys) or self-running (played back as a movie).

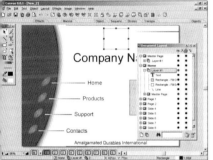

7

Some graphics packages can generate distributable slideshows if they offer a frame-based mode or animation editing features. Here we're working on a slide presentation in Deneba Canvas, using a fairly standard Web page-style template.

8

In the Save As dialogue window, it's a simple matter of choosing the Canvas Slide Show file type.

9

This generates a completely self-contained ".exe" program that plays your presentation on any PC; no additional player software is required.

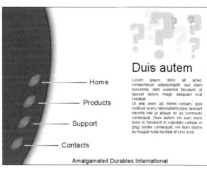

31

You can aid navigation by labeling each page, screen, or slide, and grouping the slide show into sub-sections. The contents should be made available as a clickable "jump list" so that your viewers can get to the portions that interest them. Many such formats provide built-in bookmarks, as do certain page-based document formats that you may not have considered using for presentations, such as Adobe Acrobat's PDF. One of the most convenient formats is HTML.

ADDING MULTIMEDIA

Sound and animation effects are thorny issues for the modern designer. As part of an interface rather than part of actual content, multimedia has very little practical purpose. It can slow down computer performance without adding any obvious value. It even risks your work appearing kitschy or amateurish. But herein lies the dilemma: people tend to expect multimedia interfaces more and more these days.

So what is a multimedia interface? It's one that incorporates sound and motion—when, for example, on-screen buttons appear to be pushed in when you click on them, the background music changes for each page, or you get audio feedback as you move the mouse pointer over links. At its worst, however, it's a mish-mash of bouncy graphics, bleeps, and pops. But done with care, you can end up with a "touchy-feely" interface that will go down well with the general public as well as being particularly appreciated by the partially sighted.

1
Microsoft Internet Explorer's button bar across the top of the program window reacts to mouse actions, rather like buttons that you might create within Web pages themselves.

2 | 3
As the mouse pointer passes over the buttons, they start to glow.

4 | 5 | 6
When you click on the buttons, they positively light up (4,5). The appearance of the buttons within the toolbar is shown in image 6.

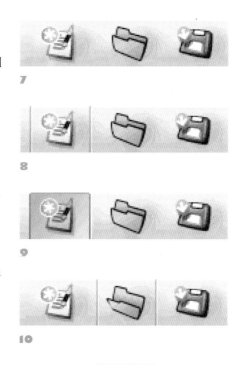

7
Netscape's Compose utility for creating Web pages provides a ribbon bar that's not just cute but animated, too, if you try it out.

8 | 9
Passing the mouse pointer over the buttons causes them to become colored and highlighted with an indented-effect square outline. Notice also how the Open Folder button appears to actually open.

10 | 11
Rather than opting for the glowy approach, Netscape pops the buttons into the shade when you click on them.

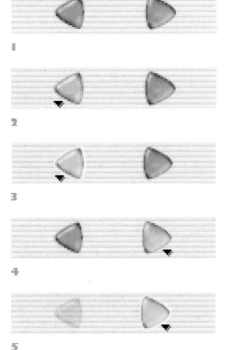

Design Directories / Series

A series of cutting-edge guides for everyone with an interest in digital design. Each book is written by an expert and deals with an area of topical interest, from colour and type for the Web, to icon and information design and web animation. All the titles offer the reader key design and technical information and tips presented in a lively, succinct way, followed by chapters showcasing the best current work in each field.

SPECIFICATION

h 235mm x **w** 210mm
w 8¼ins x **h** 9¼ins
extent 192pp 4×4
pb approx 40,000 words plus 500 pictures

interface design   www.colour   www.layout

What the whole issue comes down to is a desire to transcend the flat, two-dimensional, and ploddingly sequential nature of computer documents. By getting on-screen objects to move or sing, you create an illusion of a personable interface that appears to be more reactive to the viewer. In other words, an animated interface isn't an interactive one, but it does create an illusion of interactivity. A button that lights up when clicked feels much more tactile than a link that doesn't respond at all until the new page suddenly appears.

The key drawback to the addition of multimedia elements is that additional multimedia always demands greater memory, processor, and operating system resources. A slow or out-of-date computer will probably not be able to play these clever effects properly, or may play them out of sync. One surefire way of confusing a viewer is to have a button that doesn't react until several seconds after it has been clicked; by the time the effect started by the button starts to play, the button will have been clicked by the user another five times in frustration. Also, if your interface is delivered over the Web, you need to juggle with file sizes to ensure its availability to those connecting with slow modems. For all your design efforts, some people despise multimedia over the Web; many technical users actually switch off graphics altogether or still use text-only browsers.

The big advantage of multimedia interfaces is that they reinforce your interface concepts. An interface that visually and audibly responds to viewers' actions should be easier for them to pick up and understand.

33

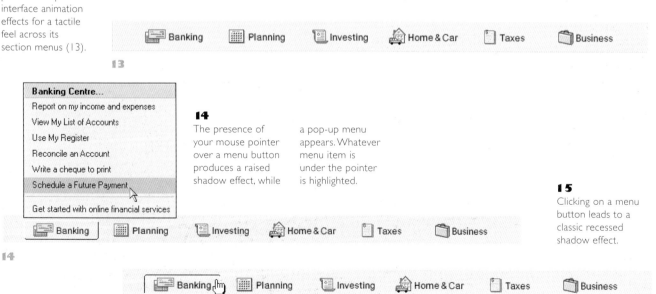

12 | 13
Quicken Deluxe (12), a personal accounts package for PCs, presents simple interface animation effects for a tactile feel across its section menus (13).

14
The presence of your mouse pointer over a menu button produces a raised shadow effect, while a pop-up menu appears. Whatever menu item is under the pointer is highlighted.

15
Clicking on a menu button leads to a classic recessed shadow effect.

INTERACTIVITY

Interactivity is a much misused term. As a designer, you must distinguish between the false claims and genuine potential of the concept. You should not waste time creating an interactive interface that isn't actually interactive, as people will soon find you out.

If the viewer just makes a text selection and then obtains a response, that cannot really be classified as interactive. Clicking an on-screen button doesn't qualify; if it did, so would turning on the ignition in a car. Interactivity is supposed to be a two-way thing. Two people having a conversation is interactive, but a quiz master asking questions and a contestant answering them isn't (unless the answer affects the nature of the next question). Internet chat is interactive, but using an Internet search engine isn't. WebTV and on-demand digital teletext services aren't interactive either. As far as interfaces are concerned, all you can do is enhance the illusion of interactivity by making the interface respond in an apparently customized way to user actions.

One way of doing this is to add multimedia effects (see page 32). Another is to fire prompts back to the viewers. A dialogue window doesn't feel interactive, but a series of quick on-screen questions may. It's a cheap trick, though, and obviously slows down your interface, so make sure you use it with care.

Yet another illusion of interactivity is achieved by giving certain types of content user-controllable, three-dimensional realism. If your site is set up to sell cars, you can allow the user to make choices and end up with a photo of the vehicle they really want. But if that vehicle is a 3D model that can be revolved in space and lets them open its doors and explore its interior, the whole experience becomes more "interactive." Of course, there's nothing interactive about shoving a ready-made 3D model under someone's nose, but it's the illusion you're after. (For more detailed information on animations and 3D solutions, see pages 96–123).

1
Visitors to the Roald Dahl Web site are greeted and led through the pages by a character from one of his books. But instead of presenting a list of the names available, the site gets children to pick their favorite character from a cartoon wheel of fortune. The result is the same, but the presentation feels more interactive.

2 | 3
WebTV technology mixes standard TV broadcast feeds with graphically rich HTML-based visuals in order to offer a more interactive presentation. While watching the news, for example, a viewer can call up additional information and browse other stories, then click through to related Web sites.

34

4

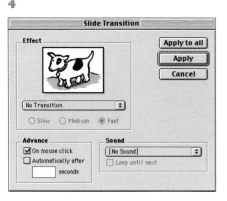

6

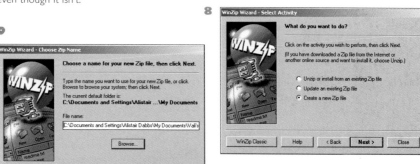

6

Compression utility WinZip offers a standard "Classic" interface and a "Wizard" interface as options. In Classic mode, you just drop files into the program window to compress them. But notice the Wizard button at the end of the iconized ribbon bar.

7

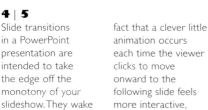

4 | 5

Slide transitions in a PowerPoint presentation are intended to take the edge off the monotony of your slideshow. They wake up the audience to the fact that you've just moved onto another slide. But when a viewer is playing back a presentation that has been distributed on CD or on-line, these transition effects can seem positively delightful. The very fact that a clever little animation occurs each time the viewer clicks to move onward to the following slide feels more interactive, even though it isn't.

8

9

10

7 | 8 | 9 | 10

Clicking on the Wizard button switches the user to Wizard mode, which takes the computer user through a sequence of fully explained steps, resulting in the compression of some files. The Wizard takes longer and doesn't offer any more options than Classic mode (in fact it offers fewer), but it exists to aid learning and give the user what appears to be a more interactive experience.

5

THE WEB EXPLOSION

The rapid expansion of the Internet in recent years has redefined the nature of all computer interfaces. For better or worse, the average interface designer can no longer afford to ignore the impact of the World Wide Web on interface design.

Before the Web took off, every custom-designed interface largely depended on a good deal of custom-made coding. Serious designers would work with C++ programmers to produce unique multimedia-based but platform-dependent programs, or use Macromedia Director or AuthorWare to produce similar results on proprietary but platform-independent technologies. Presentation packages came with a so-called "runtime" player program so that viewers could play the presentations back on their own machines. All these systems still exist, but the Web has made things a lot simpler by becoming the preferred non-proprietary, multi-platform interface layer of choice.

Since Web browsers are found on practically all computers, notebooks, handhelds, and even many mobile phones, getting to grips with modern interface design involves learning how to create HTML. Web standards work off-line as well as on-line and so are gradually being incorporated into interfaces for everything from parking lot ticket dispensers to domestic refrigerators. The extensive customizability of Web pages makes them the ideal springboard for interface design.

You also need to be aware of the effect that the Web has had upon the way people use electronic equipment. The Web itself is not an identifiable location of the Internet, but is rather an umbrella name for HTML pages; it's the nature of the hypertext links on these pages that make them a "web." Clicking from link to link, or jumping from site to site in succession, is known as "surfing." The most often-clicked on-screen button in computing today is the "Back" button, which is found in Web, file, and graphics browsers.

1
Here's the Web as we most often know it: in a large window, on a fast computer, using lots of graphics. It's a veritable storefront. But the full impact of the Web is now being felt across a variety of computerized devices, many of which are handheld.

2
If you want attractive layouts on these palmtops, consider reformatting the site for AvantGo. This system lets viewers download an off-line packaged version of your site. Here is the same story prepared for and viewed with AvantGo. Note how it lets you keep the site branding up front.

36

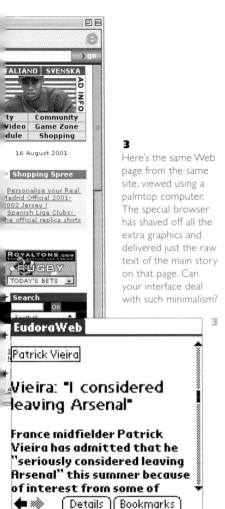

3

Here's the same Web page from the same site, viewed using a palmtop computer. The special browser has shaved off all the extra graphics and delivered just the raw text of the main story on that page. Can your interface deal with such minimalism?

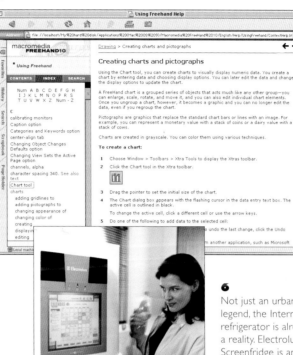

5

HTML is fast taking over the old hyperlink systems for reference documents such as Help files supplied with application software. Web standards also allow you to design these Help files to be visually appealing. The navigation buttons, logos, and tabs here are all the product of a designer, not a programmer.

6

Not just an urban legend, the Internet refrigerator is already a reality. Electrolux's Screenfridge is an otherwise upright fridge with a Web connection and LCD color screen on the door. The idea is that you can use it to order groceries on-line, but it can also be used for surfing while you happen to be in the kitchen—the ultimate fridge magnet, if you like. It won't be long before Web design will need to embrace all kinds of everyday utility devices like this.

4

Just for good measure, this is what the same site looks like from a WAP mobile phone. Again, the site will need re-formatting specifically for WAP if you want it to look right, include appropriate graphics, and so on.

In other words, people no longer plod along a menu in a sequential fashion if they can help it. An interface needs to let the viewer surf and get back to where they were. It needs to work on varying screen sizes and different computers. It may need to operate in multiple windows. It is also expected to look good. Thankfully, you no longer have to shred tags and code in order to produce good HTML. All mainstream design software packages can now generate Web graphic elements, animations, or even entire pages and interconnected sites. Over the next three chapters, we'll look at graphics, navigation, and animation as key interface issues, with constant reference to Web standards.

WHY IMAGERY? • 40

LAYOUT PRINCIPLES • 42

ICON DESIGN • 44

THUMBNAILS • 46

BACKGROUNDS • 48

SKINS AND OVERLAYS • 50

LOGICAL OVERHEADS • 52

TECHNICAL OVERHEADS • 54

COLOR CONSISTENCY • 56

COLOR MANAGEMENT • 60

TYPOGRAPHY • 64

LEGIBILITY • 66

CROSS-PLATFORM TYPE • 68

OTHER VISUAL CLUES • 70

ROGUE'S GALLERY • 72

38

WHY IMAGERY?

The very concept of modern on-screen user interfaces centers around graphics. But this hasn't always been the case. Some of the early postwar computers needed to be "programmed" with cogs and they then responded with calculation results displayed as variously illuminated lamps. Then came punched cards and responses delivered on continuous dot-matrix printouts. Next, computers in the 1970s were considered to boast the cutting edge of interface design by employing a text-based question-and-answer routine, handled on-screen.

To a degree, the 1970s computer designers were right. As books and newspapers have demonstrated for hundreds of years, nothing gets information across as efficiently or clearly as black text on a white page … or in the case of early computers, white (or sometimes green) text on a black background. It's no wonder that the field of presentation graphics actually includes "text chart" as its most important type of slide, miles ahead of bar charts and pie charts. So isn't the fad for graphically rich interfaces just that—a fad? It depends upon the difference between content and presentation. Content needs to be presented, otherwise no one can get access to it: even raw text needs to be legible. Today's world of sound bites and fast delivery emphasizes the need for information to be presented in a way that can be received easily by an audience that is no longer prepared to put great effort into reception. For example, the broadsheet format for tabloid newspaper page sizes was ditched in the 1960s to make it easier to read them spread on kitchen tables or while on public transporation. This was purely an interface upgrade.

40

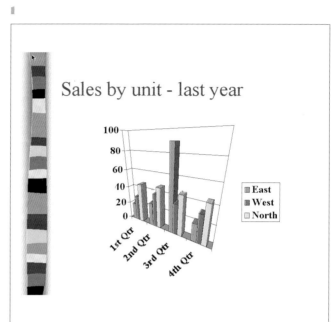

Sales by unit - last year

1 | 2
Information can speak for itself when it is presented graphically. More to the point, specific information and key ideas are more easily understood in graphic terms, especially when surrounded by less important, distracting data. So while the table of figures (2) provides the actual results of a business, it's only when it's presented as a chart (1) that a viewer notices how significant the Eastern sector's performance was in the third quarter.

Sales by unit - last year

	1st Qtr	2nd Qtr	3rd Qtr	4th Qtr
East	20.4	27.4	90	20.4
West	30.6	38.6	34.6	31.6
North	45.9	46.9	45	43.9

2

3

Shakespeare's sonnets

radical skateboard

Live gigs at the Warehouse

TRADITIONAL VALUES

How to fill in your tax form

Just as tabloid pages have less space than broadsheets, the shrinking size of computer screens forces interface designers to be even more succinct in the way they present content. A picture may not always paint a thousand words, but imagery saves space by summarizing complex commands and ideas into visual objects. Think icons. Think descriptions. And, not least, think how simple it is to replace the words, "Click here to move on from this screen to the next screen," with a little picture of an arrow pointing to the right.

41

3
Type is a form of graphic, and can be used and misused accordingly. As you can see, the look of fonts suggests a purpose, character, or era, and we've deliberately chosen here a few examples that are incongruous to the subject matter. Unless this is your intent, such misuse will confuse the viewer.

4 | 5 | 6
You can learn a lot from children's multimedia titles, which are required to employ graphic means to back up spoken instructions every time. When children want to exit the program, they will be asked to click on an appropriate graphic button as confirmation. However, note how the use of color (the classic stop-go of red and green) is used inconsistently across the examples shown here. Which button would you click on to exit?

LAYOUT PRINCIPLES

Interface design can learn much from print design, even though issues such as multimedia and physical hardware present their own special challenges. This is because digital interfaces generally follow the page format. There is a screen that contains structured information, and this screen can be expanded, scrolled, or replaced by another page-style screenful. Because this screen is relatively small, comparisons with the approach color magazines take are obvious. So to successfully work within a screen, you can follow the layout principles of magazine design.

First, every page needs a focus. Viewers want to know where to look first, so they want to be clearly shown which piece of information is the most important on the page. This can be indicated by the size, color, and amount of space given to the information or by the position of it on the page, as well as by how it's framed by the other content that is located around it.

Next, you need to understand the order in which people will probably look at various objects on the page. People generally look at pictures first, especially if they are large, have striking content, or have been treated in a special way (such as being "cut out"). Then they might look at the captions to those pictures for clues as to what the story and page are supposed to be about. Headlines come next, providing the viewers with yet more clues. Then it will be pull-quotes and anything put in bold type, such as an opening sentence or paragraph, that draws their attention. Finally, if you're very lucky, they might just start reading the text content.

1
Let's suppose that you are laying out three stories in a desktop publishing program. The simple way to do it—as seen in thousands of club newsletters—is to run the text over columns and insert the headlines and pictures where appropriate. Design issues aside, this is actually the kind of layout that people least like to read.

2
Take the same page and make the stories independent, working horizontally rather than vertically. Because the columns are shorter, people believe there's less to read. Note how headlining and picture size tells you which of the stories is the most important one. Its position also creates a focus for the eye on the page.

You should also remember that, with the exception of certain scripts such as traditional Japanese and Cantonese, people always read horizontally. This means that they will find landscape-shaped content more comfortable to read. This is extremely important for interface design, since the screen is very often landscape-shaped, too. Viewers hate to scroll; they may scroll downward, but they hate scrolling back up to find all the bits and pieces that vanished off the screen since they began scrolling.

People, generally speaking, are also more likely to have the patience to read short volumes of text than copious numbers of paragraphs or pages. It's not that they necessarily stop reading after a certain number of words, but long passages may well end up not being read at all. Viewers can, however, usually be easily persuaded to read lots of short text columns rather than one or two very long ones. This tip applies to both text and graphics, and is a very appropriate way of avoiding the scroll factor.

3 | 4
Now see these techniques in action on the Web at MSNBC (3) and Yahoo (4). Although these pages are packed with links and graphic elements, each has an area of focus that grabs the viewer before anything else. Pictures don't just illustrate a story, they tell you where to look.

5

Stripping a page-based interface to the bone, this is how people see your content.
1. Pictures grab the attention first, although this depends upon their placement, of course.
2. If the picture is interesting or not self-explanatory, viewers might check out the caption.
3. Any pull-quotes or areas of bold intro text give viewers an idea of what the page is all about.

4. Having got this far, viewers might actually read the page heading.
5. Assuming you've grabbed their interest with all this, viewers turn to the body text, but may still only read the first sentence or two.
6. If your viewers are bored, they'll look for other links, typically on the left.
7. To be honest, the chance of very casual visitors looking up here at all is remote, but it can happen.

43

ICON DESIGN

As we discovered on page 18, icons are the ultimate conceptual graphic within a digital interface. These little pictures can represent programs and documents, for example, as well as reveal what kind of programs or documents they are, their current status, their capability, and so on.

But even if you're not creating original software applications, you can use icon-style conceptual graphics as part of any interface. Let's say you have designed a presentation to include triggers and links for external file formats, such as Acrobat PDFs, QuickTime movies, and MP3 audio. By using recognizable file icons for these formats as their trigger buttons, you save a lot of screen space while also providing a familiar set of tools for the everyday computer user. For example, this user may have no idea what a PDF file is, but may well recognize the Acrobat file icon. Similarly, many people will be left scratching their heads when a Web page contains a link to an FTP site, but will understand the concept readily if the link button is a simple folder icon.

44

Sound Card Drivers

Address: file:///My%20hard%20disk/Desktop%20Folder/Temporary$$$.html

Company-Name	Device(s)	Description	Driver
Acer	Magic S20, S22, and MP23 Sound Cards	Get updated drivers from their FTP site	
Avance Logic	Avance Logic sound cards	Get updated drivers from their FTP site	
Aria	Aria Sound Card	Get updated drivers for digital and extended MIDI from their FTP site	
Aztech Labs	Clinton, Nova, Washington, and other Sound Cards	Get updated drivers from their FTP site	
Boca Research	Sound Expression, and Voyager Movie Player Card	Get current drivers from their Web site	
Cardinal Technologies	DSP Sound and SNAPlus Capture Boards	Get current drivers from their BBS, or you may try their Web site	
Creative Labs	SoundBlaster and VideoBlaster Family	Get current drivers from their Web site	
Crystal Semiconductor	CS4232 Sound Card	Get current drivers from their Web site	
Diamond Multimedia	Stealth Video, Viper Video, and Other Cards	Get current drivers from their Web site	
Digital Audio Labs	Audio I/O Adapters	Get current drivers from their Web site	
ELSA	WINNER Graphic Boards	Get current drivers from their FTP site	

Local machine zone

1

It's not essential to use graphics in this list of software downloads, but by using a set of simple icons rather than just hyperlinked text in the final column, you're giving the viewer an idea of which links lead to FTP sites and which lead to Web pages.

2 | 3 | 4 | 5

As mentioned in the first chapter, icons are supposed to represent graphically what the object is or does. While there's room to be very clever here, some of the most useful icons are the plainest and most self-explanatory.

6 | 7 | 8 | 9

When embedding links to multimedia playback file formats, it is good to use the format's own icons as link buttons to demonstrate what each link does. Many icons are familiar to users; even those that aren't are fairly self-evident, if only because of the triangular Play symbol within the icon itself.

2　　　3　　　4　　　5　　　6　　　7

4

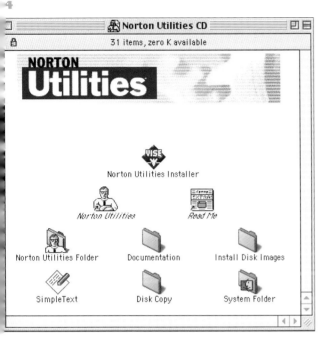

When distributing self-running presentations, custom icons can help you to emphasize your branding. A special icon can also make your presentation stand out from the mass of icons on a user's desktop. This can be critical if your presentation is to be downloaded from a Web site or delivered by email: once it has landed on the desktop, can the user find it or will it be lost?

Custom icons are popular resources on all computing platforms, both as interface-wide themes and as individual icon replacements. On the Mac, designers have used structured icon layouts within folders to create a basic interface that doesn't require any program. Company logos and instructions can be presented by preparing icons as jigsaw puzzle pieces. Even in Windows, icon appearance can tell people what to do, thereby visually reinforcing what the files in a folder are for and which program is supposed to be run first.

45

5

14 | 15
The icon precision of the Mac platform allows designers to create logo splash screens right within folders on the desktop. The Norton Utilities logo (14) in this folder view, for example, is actually made up of a virtual jigsaw of 22 carefully aligned icons (15).

10 | 11 | 12 | 13
Buttons that carry out an action can be given icons to represent that action. It's not as difficult as you might think, | although many designers resort to putting text inside the picture as an extra clue. Can you work out which of these icons represents a | set-up program, an exit action, a copy action, and a program that converts Acrobat PDFs into Palm handheld format?

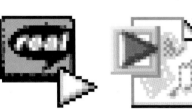

8   **9**   **10**   **11**   **12**   **13**

THUMBNAILS

An alternative to the conceptual graphic is the representational graphic. Instead of encapsulating the nature and potential of a file into a little picture, a miniature version of the information contained within a file is shown, in order to indicate what the file will look like when it has been opened.

The latest versions of Windows and the Mac OS provide thumbnails when the user is browsing files and folders. When you click on a file icon, within a couple of seconds you will see a thumbnail representation of what that particular file looks like. This thumbnail is shown in a special "file info" pane in the browsing window. The one problem is that this feature can only deal with the first page in a multi-page file, so it pays to ensure that your first page is clear and representative. In other words, if you are designing a document that is intended for distribution, make sure that the first page is a killer and let the viewer's operating system do the rest of the work for you.

Certain software packages support proprietary thumbnail previews of their particular file formats. Browsing files within Microsoft Office programs, for example, allows you to check thumbnails of what's inside Word, Excel, and PowerPoint documents without actually having to open them up. Again, bear this in mind when you are distributing files in these formats— tweak the appearance of initial pages so that they look good as thumbnails.

Within a full interface, such as a multimedia title or booth program, you can use thumbnails as miniature representations of link pages and other relevant documents. These tell the viewer more about what they're linking to than icons alone ever could. Thumbnails are typically bigger than icons, and can present more detail about actual content—such as whether the link points to a picture, a text document, a game, or whatever.

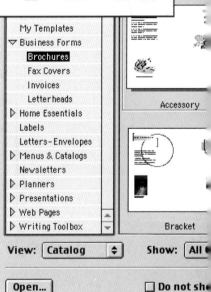

1 | 2
Modern operating systems support on-the-fly thumbnail previews. This means that you can browse a folder on the desktop and obtain an instant preview of what the document (or just its first page) looks like or sounds like. If you have control over the development of an entire multimedia project, then this "instant thumbnail" system is worth emulating.

3
Microsoft Office presents a Project Gallery interface for users wanting to create a new document based on template layouts and content. The key to making the Project Gallery worthwhile is its thumbnail views of each template. Consider how a similar approach might suit an interface in which you want to let viewers jump to other pages of your slide show, sections of your Web site, categories in your database, and so on.

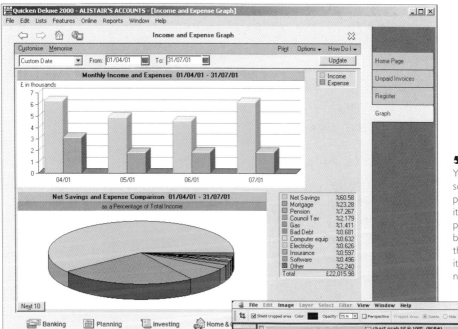

5
You can make a screen grab of the program and open it up in a graphics package. Crop into a bold, clear element in the image, then save it in the program's native file format.

47

4
Let's say that you have a document that contains financial information, but you've spotted this histogram graphic in a completely unrelated program.

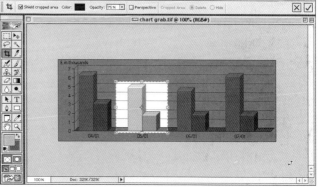

5

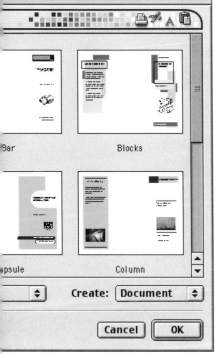

6
Without any extra effort, the program has generated its own little file icon for the graphic you have just saved.

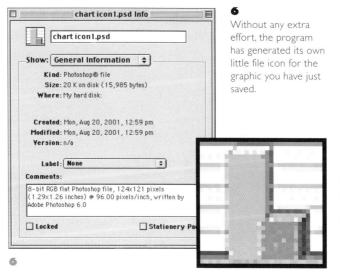

7
The icon can then be easily copied and reused for any other file, by pasting it into the icon box in its 'Get Info' dialogue box.

6

7

BACKGROUNDS

When companies order letterhead for their official correspondence, they often look at paper color and texture, and they may even consider putting watermarks or subliminal printed elements across every sheet. A blank sheet of paper is viewed as an opportunity to reinforce branding and produce immediate recognition. Similar opportunities are open to you when you are designing interfaces.

A special background behind your digital content can actually serve many other purposes rather than just showing a company logo. A background can be used to add interest or depth to flat, colorless page-based information. An obvious example of this is the classic gradient tint background to business presentations. Another example is "wallpaper" graphics behind Web pages. In either case, you must remember that backgrounds are supposed to stay in the background and not interfere with the content at the front.

Another use for backgrounds is to provide a graphical layout that would otherwise be monotonous to prepare as many individual elements. For example, your interface might feature a panel of menu options or sub-sections down the left-hand side of the screen. Instead of building the panel as a separate object, you can create an illusion of the same thing by using a background that

1
If you insist on placing a tiled, textured background behind text, you risk your text becoming illegible. Test the effect out in advance yourself or at a graphics Web site such as www.WebPage Background.com, which is shown here. The results can often be surprising.

6

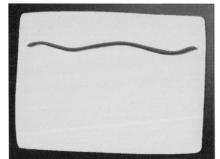

7

2 | 3 | 4
You don't need to admire the layout to appreciate the color coding at work on this Web site. Each tab across the top represents a themed micro-site. The tab colors are then also used throughout those micro-sites, working as a reminder of where you are.

5 | 6 | 7 | 8
It's traditional for projector presentations to be designed with dark backgrounds so that the overlaid text can stand out as white, yellow, or another brilliant color. Just be warned that desktop presentations on a computer tend to look odd with dark backgrounds.

8

contains a colored patch sitting behind that left-hand area. Taking this approach further, the background could incorporate colored patches across the top, too, which have been designed to line up with other links. Then as the viewer moves from page to page, all that's changing is the content layer—the background remains the same. Not only does this mean less work for you, but the pages should load more quickly for your viewer, too.

You can extend this approach to accommodate multiple backgrounds that represent different moods or sections of your content. For example, your interface might feature color-coded tab selections for different areas of a Web site or for different topics in a training movie. As the viewer moves into a particular area, the background colors provide a visual clue as to which area it is. Telling viewers where they are, and not just where to go or where they've just been, is an important element in interface navigation (see pages 74–95).

SKINS AND OVERLAYS

A "skin" is a graphical interface "overcoat" dropped onto an existing program. It is an extension of the concept that the core function of a piece of software and its user interface are separate items. Windows, title bars, icons, and so on are just window dressing from a programmer's point of view. They are all merely elements that can be customized or altered to suit.

At operating-system level, you can customize things yourself by choosing different color and typeface themes. These are simple overlays that can be used to aid usability or add a bit of fun. You could build a theme called "amphibian" featuring green text, watery noises, and a wallpaper background image of a frog. However, this theme is still just an overlay, and could actually hinder rather than enhance the interface.

Skins go further by hooking into the functions of a particular program. If you know that the program supports a specific set of functions and commands, you can design the buttons or even the whole interface. The program in question needs to support skins in the first place, but you may be surprised how many actually do. Obvious examples include various MP3 audio utilities, but certain Web browsers can be re-skinned, too.

50

4

5

1

2

3

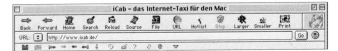

1 | 2 | 3
Some packages, such as the Web browser iCab, allow limited customization of the main tool bar and animated graphics. You might offer personalized graphics as a promotional item, by overlaying a commercial program's interface with your own.

4 | 5
Netscape's Web browser is even more customizable than iCab, supporting a more general interface enhancement. This means that you can change the background and window style, for example, as well as the buttons.

Creating custom skins can be tricky, and you'll need to
obtain special software utilities that may be provided by
the program's creator. These are often made available
free of charge in the hope that your skins will add value
to the original product by making it more attractive to
buyers. In return, you get the opportunity to make
someone else's program "your own" with a custom
interface that demonstrates your skills to potential
clients, boosts an overall theme you're trying to
establish, or slams home some commercial branding.

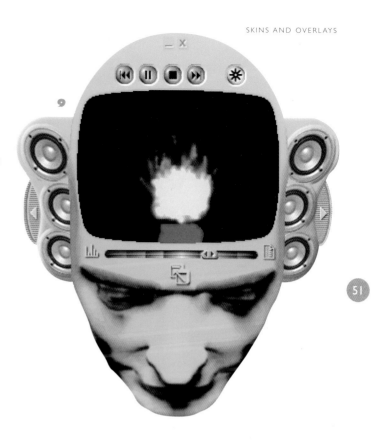

51

6 | 7 | 8
Operating systems
can also be themed,
as is seen here with
Windows. Some
consumer-oriented
businesses have
produced and
distributed themes to
the general public
based around their
products.

9 | 10 | 11
Because of their
focus on consumers,
media player utilities
often support add-in
skins that completely
alter the character of
the on-screen
interface. Here's
Windows Media
Player in three
different guises.

LOGICAL OVERHEADS

Playing around with pictures and other graphical elements can have an extremely detrimental effect on an interface if you're not careful. Esthetic design issues aside, the most common error made in graphical interfaces is the presentation of too much visual information in one go. Remember when I said earlier that interface designers could learn a lot from print designers? Well, this is an example: a screenful of junk is no more likely to succeed than a printed page full of junk. Viewers need a focus for their attention and must be led through an interface with clear visual clues, rather than being confused by a mass of graphics that are all fighting for their attention.

There is an old adage in editorial circles that demands "illustration, not decoration." While there are cross-over situations where a bit of both goes down nicely, you should always keep in mind that graphic elements in an interface are supposed to serve functional purposes. Looking pretty isn't necessarily one of them, especially if you are preparing them in isolation from the rest of the interface.

For example, buttons may link to other screens, launch programs, or trigger actions, but they should also, at the same time, suggest what those links, etc., might be. It's all too easy to spend hours designing a button to look like a 3D lightbulb when in fact the thing the button is going to link to has nothing to do with

1 | 2
There isn't a point at which there are "too many" or "too few" images in an interface that supports graphics. Use the design brief to create an interface that suits a purpose, an audience, and, of course, the hardware it's going to run on. Google (1) is stark because it has a reputation for speed; Cartoon Network's (2) site is dazzling to attract young viewers.

3 | 4 | 5
Often misunderstood, graphics can actually do your WAP site the world of good. Not only do they reinforce branding and remind viewers where in the site they are, these graphics are also very sma[ll] and add an insignificant amount of waiting time when downloading to a mobile phone.

3

4

5

6

The multimedia title *How Animals Move* demonstrates how to keep an interface clean while at the same time filling it with images. Highlighted button areas overlay this countryside scene. When you click on a button, it animates, and then a more functional label appears.

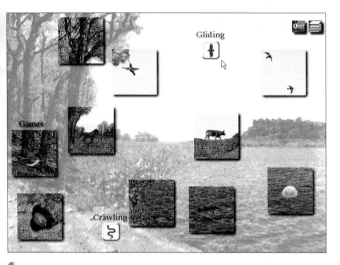

6

7

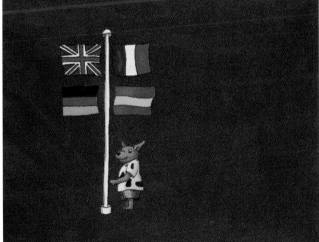

7 | 8

Is your interface likely to be presented in more than one language? A drop-down list of country names (7) is impractical, since the names we use in English are rarely the same as those used in other languages. Instead, try using a small national flag (8) as a link to the relevant foreign-language interface.

8

lightbulbs. It may seem predictable, but there's a good reason why international Web sites use country flags as button links to different language pages. It might be amusing to turn all your Forward and Back buttons into pine trees at Christmas, but you can't beat the plain arrow symbols for sheer clarity.

There is still an argument for decoration, as long as it is used in the proper context: Christmas trees can be employed here and there if the design is carried out with discretion and if the theme is relevant. But again, this only works if they serve a function by being there. In this case, they may tell viewers that an e-commerce site is hosting a Christmas sale or, at the very least, be used to inform a viewer that a presentation held in late December is up-to-date. Just be sure that the theme does not take over from the interface and sidetrack the content that you really want to get across.

TECHNICAL OVERHEADS

The one big advantage that print designers enjoy over digital interface designers is the freedom from the constraints of computer performance. A glossy color magazine needs no more effort to pick up than a golf club newsletter does. However, digital information is much more susceptible to what has been placed on the pages—especially if a lot of graphical information has been packed into the design.

Quite simply, the more complex the design, the more effort a computer will have to make to present it. In the wider world of interface design, you must remember that these computers can be anything from dumb LCD readouts to mobile phones, not just state-of-the-art PCs and Macs. The mobile phone example is especially valid these days: you can enhance WAP pages with title graphics, but if you overdo them, then each page will load slowly and clumsily. After a couple of stumbling page loads, especially if the network reception is poor and therefore even slower than usual, a viewer will give up and go to a faster-loading competitor's site instead.

54

1
This image is 150 pixels wide and 172 pixels high, which makes it around 2 x 2.5in (5 x 6.25cm) when displayed on-screen at 72dpi. It's fairly typical of a graphic that you might incorporate into a multimedia interface, Web site, or presentation. But the original file in TIFF format is 77.6Kb, which is a little large if you want lots of similar images to load up on-screen at the same time, and it is certainly too big for Web graphics.

2
Here we've converted the image to JPEG format, with a reasonable 80 percent quality setting. The resulting file is just 4.9Kb in size.

3
Now here it is again as a GIF image, using a palette of just 128 different colors. This version is 11.2Kb.

4
Finally, here it is as a PNG file, again with a 128-color palette. The image comes out at 9.8Kb.

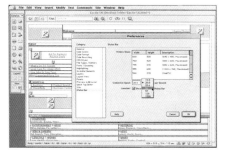

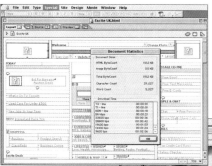

7 | 8 | 9
Mainstream graphics software includes optimization utilities when saving to certain image file formats. Here you can see Macromedia Fireworks (7), Deneba Canvas (8) and Adobe ImageReady (9) reprocess TIFF photo images as GIFs, JPEGs, and PNGs

The same principle works for all sort of things, from PowerPoint presentations and in-house training materials to Flash-enhanced Web sites. Your interface is a slave to the processing power of the computer on which it's run. This is exactly as it should be. All too often, viewers end up being a slave to the interface, which is the number one reason that they switch off and look elsewhere.

Professional Web design studios work according to in-house rules, such as a maximum size for any single Web page. These rules may be based on a particular modem speed using a certain Internet access provider.

Business-to-business and educational sites might have a ceiling of 20Kb per page; commercial sites might push this to 50Kb or more and include Macromedia Flash animations as well. You should establish such rules for your own work. Even a simple business presentation might end up being played on an old computer with insufficient memory.

55

5 | 6
Web design packages, such as Macromedia Dreamweaver (5) and Adobe GoLive (6) shown here, provide instant reports on overall document sizes as you work. This is translated into download speeds according to the class of Internet connection a viewer has. So, although many designers create sites with 56K modems in mind, it's interesting to see how much longer someone will have to wait for your pages to download if they only have an old 28.8K modem—or indeed an ISDN line.

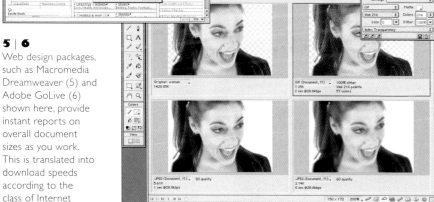

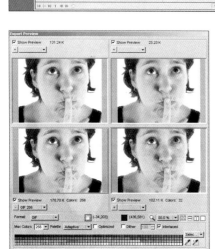

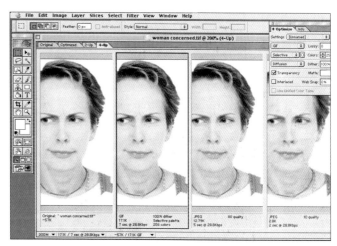

8

9

COLOR CONSISTENCY

Intelligent use of color is practiced by designers worldwide. The idea is to create consistency and recognition using a small number of harmonious colors. The result isn't necessarily hard-hitting, but it's important that your interface follows these rules. The viewers shouldn't notice the interface first: they should be looking at the content. Design novices often splash around with primaries, which can lead to hideous results. With a lot of information presented in reds, blues, and yellows, viewers won't know where to look.

Most design software allows you to work with a user-defined, limited selection of colors. Some Web-oriented design packages even provide a library of color palettes, which comprises sets of harmonious colors. These are highly recommended for self-taught designers, as the choices are based on tried-and-tested mixtures. You just apply the colors: you don't have to think too hard about whether one item is going to clash with another, as it will be really obvious if it does happen. In a professional scenario, you'll negotiate these palettes with your client. They will be based on corporate logo colors and may tie into existing printed literature.

Color consistency can also be employed as a navigational aid. Increasingly dark shades, for example, might reflect a viewer's progression through a sequence of screens. Whether you use ready-made palettes or create your own, give them useful names and then keep them safe, as you will probably use them again. You may wish to establish cross-range tones that can be reproduced on-screen and in print, in order to ensure consistency if your client asks for a complete design job.

1 | 2 | 3

Microsoft Publisher incorporates a color coordination system for its templates and wizards that self-taught designers might appreciate. Whether you're creating a printed page, Web page, or presentation, you can switch the color scheme for the entire document with one click. Of course, this only works if you stick to the preset color styles to start with.

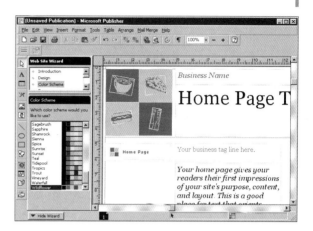

4

In order to maintain color consistency in a design package, you would normally prepare a custom coordinated set in the Color palette and then try to use only those colors. So although GoLive's palette here lets you work with a whole range of color spaces, it's the restricted set that you'll probably use the most in Web design.

5

Things are rather more automated in PowerPoint, and it offers similar functionality as Publisher does, as the color scheme you choose can be switched halfway through the job. Schemes are chosen and applied from PowerPoint's Formatting Palette.

6

To create additional color schemes in PowerPoint, you just edit the Color Scheme dialogue. The different objects on the slides are already named as styles as part of the program: you just choose the colors.

4

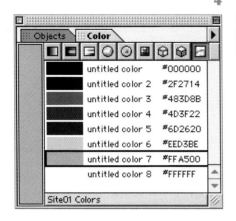

5

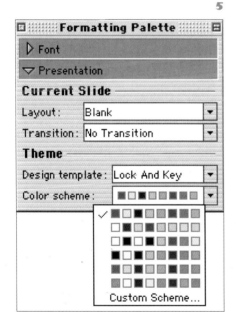

6

7

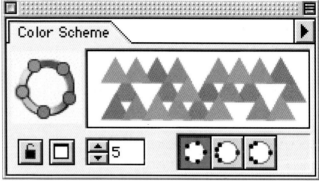

8

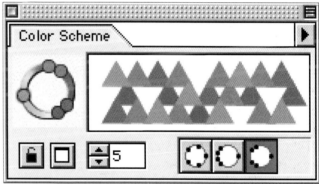

9

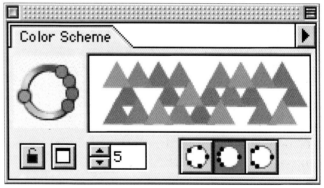

7 | 8 | 9

Adobe LiveMotion provides a special Color Scheme palette if you are working with vector animations. It uses a coordination system based on plot points on a color wheel. Many professional designers already use this approach to establish harmonious colors, and it is definitely handy to have it built into your creative software.

COLOR CONSISTENCY II

Maintaining harmonious colors between principal objects—text, panels, buttons—isn't difficult, but the addition of pictures can threaten the whole design. There's not a lot you can do about a photograph that contains colors that clash wildly with the rest of your interface. For professionals, photography is one element within the design brief; pictures will be commissioned to match the established palette. Anything that doesn't look quite right can still be adjusted in a photo-editing package. You can emulate this if you don't have control over the images you include in your layouts. The cheapest and easiest trick of all is to make black-and-white photographs "house style." You can then tint these black-and-white images with one of your palette colors so that they employ the tones you're using elsewhere. The biggest problems occur with background graphics

or wallpaper images. Used without restraint, wallpaper will clash with everything, so backgrounds are best kept simple. Use a single flat color, a handful of well-demarcated adjacent flat colors, or linear gradients from a single color through to black.

Of course, graphics have their functional element, too. Clashing colors may actually serve your purpose. Bright reds and greens wouldn't normally be run side by side, but they are just what you'd want for a Christmas theme. The trick is to stick with the same reds and greens.

3

Now you can re-color the images with Pantone 471 using the paint and tint tools in your graphics package. We're using Photoshop, so it's a simple matter of applying the Duotone command, reducing the black to a gray, and adding the house brown color to the mix.

1
Let's assume that the house style for your interface is Pantone 471 (brown) but that you have to accommodate these two brightly colored images.

2
The first step is to convert them both to grayscale. Then adjust the highlight and shadow points so that they are equally matched.

4
The result: you've lost that nice color, but at least the images won't look out of place with your interface—or with each other.

5

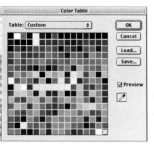

256 colors

6

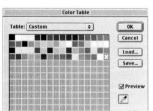

128 colors

5 | 6 | 7 | 8 | 9 | 10 | 11

Optimizing a graphic for fast display in a presentation or for fast downloading on a Web page can cause problems with color consistency. Each progressive level of optimization forces your graphics software to discard more colors or detail, in turn risking the whole picture becoming out of whack with the rest of your interface. See for yourself how the palette changes as we restrict the options on the color table.

59

7

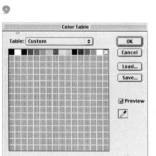

64 colors

8

32 colors

9

16 colors

10

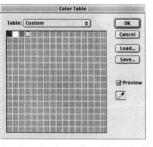

8 colors

11

4 colors (having relinquished black)

COLOR MANAGEMENT

In real life, color is perceived as analog light wavelengths by the retina, which then sends signals to the brain. Color on a computer is perceived in exactly the same way. What differs is the generation of the colors to start with. In real life, colors are made up of natural dyes and pigments and are tempered by surface textures, translucence, and shapes, not to mention ambient light temperature, brightness, and angle of viewing. Color on a computer, on the other hand, is made up of zeros and ones, as is everything else.

The problem with digital color is that it doesn't automatically take into account real-world variances. Nothing illustrates this better than walking into an electronics store and facing a dozen television screens, all showing the same channel but each with a slightly different hint to the color reproduction. Try walking up to one of the TV sets and playing with the color settings: you're not altering the color information component of the picture signal by doing this, but are simply changing the way the TV represents that color.

It is just the same with computers. A picture that looks bright on one monitor might look dark on another, or a reddish tint on-screen might look green on a projector screen. A good-looking picture might end up looking terrible when you scan it in, so you could spend hours fixing it only to find it looks even worse when viewed on another computer.

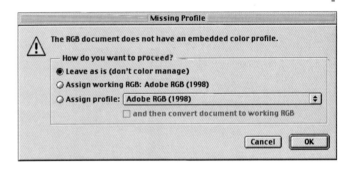

1 | 2

In professional graphics software, such as Photoshop, color management systems are built in, which means that you're forced to use them properly or face the consequences. If you didn't specify a device profile when photographing or scanning the image (2), Photoshop (1) prompts you to assign one.

3
Without color management, you risk a situation where everything looks great on-screen, but when you print the image, it comes out surprisingly flat.

4
Even with correct device profiles chosen, this won't save you if the devices themselves have been incorrectly calibrated after the profiles were created. For example, if your monitor is set too dark, you may end up over-brightening and over-saturating the image, and it will only become evident on someone else's monitor.

2

4

60

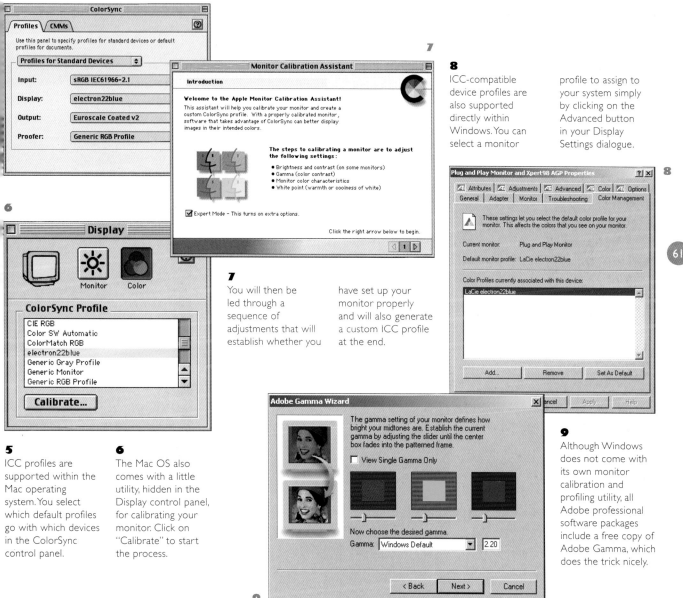

8
ICC-compatible device profiles are also supported directly within Windows. You can select a monitor profile to assign to your system simply by clicking on the Advanced button in your Display Settings dialogue.

7
You will then be led through a sequence of adjustments that will establish whether you have set up your monitor properly and will also generate a custom ICC profile at the end.

5
ICC profiles are supported within the Mac operating system. You select which default profiles go with which devices in the ColorSync control panel.

6
The Mac OS also comes with a little utility, hidden in the Display control panel, for calibrating your monitor. Click on "Calibrate" to start the process.

9
Although Windows does not come with its own monitor calibration and profiling utility, all Adobe professional software packages include a free copy of Adobe Gamma, which does the trick nicely.

The problem isn't necessarily that your monitors aren't set up properly, but that the different hardware devices are not capable of reproducing precisely the same range ("gamut") of colors, even though the digital information in software remains the same. To keep colors consistent from one monitor to the next, or indeed between scanners, monitors, and printers, you should establish a regime of color management. On a Mac, use the ColorSync control panel; on a PC, use the Color Management section of your Display Properties. Both color management systems work in the background and are based on so-called "ICC profiles," which help interpret digital color information to match the various devices it is being presented on.

COLOR MANAGEMENT II

B y establishing a color-managed set up, you can
improve your chances of maintaining color fidelity
when editing graphics. As long as your scanner, printer,
monitor, and projector are calibrated, you are unlikely to
find significant shifts in color when graphics are
presented or output by one or another.

This is all very well if you have the opportunity to
color-manage the ultimate output device as well. For
example, you can ensure that your digital projector is
set up correctly and that booth machines are calibrated
to display colors just as they should. But you can't
calibrate the potential millions of computers out there
that will view your graphics. Even if every owner is
running their operating system's built-in color
management system, there's no way of telling if they
have adjusted the brightness and contrast to be too low
or too high. Nor do you have any say over whether they
are viewing your interface in a sealed cellar or next to a
south-facing window at noon in the summer.

1 | 2
Differences between
the Mac standard
gamma of 1.8 and
Windows' standard of
2.2 mean that you
have to be careful
when preparing
images on one
platform when it's
going to be viewed
on both. For example,
here's a photo as
seen on a Mac (1);
compare that with
how it's seen when
brought onto a PC
running Windows (2).
The difference is
subtle, but the image
is noticeably lighter
on the Mac.

3 | 4
Further variances can
be found on other
systems that are set
to different gamma
levels, or indeed
other Macs and PCs
with poor screen

output or bad
calibration. You can't
control this situation,
but you can
compensate for it by
avoiding very dark
and very pale images.

What you can do is try to avoid extreme colors and tonal limits in your interface. Graphic elements that are very bright or dark risk getting lost altogether if they are viewed in an imperfect lighting environment—which indeed they probably will be.

There's an additional problem—PCs and Macs employ different default "gamma" settings. A gamma setting in this sense is a type of brightness-and-contrast preset, which is given as a single numeric figure rating. PCs are customarily set at gamma 2.2, while Macs typically assume gamma 1.8. The result is that graphics designed on a PC can look pale when viewed on a Mac, while those designed on a Mac end up appearing to be too dark on a PC.

Even worse, a whole host of new color-screen devices are now being used regularly for accessing interfaces that were previously only intended for desktop computers. For example, palmtops can browse the Web, run presentations, and even play back Flash movies. Digital cable and satellite customers can now surf the Internet on their TVs. This is all a color management nightmare. But what you can do is ensure that everything is at least calibrated correctly at your end, and then take steps to avoid color extremes that may push beyond the display limitations of the device being used to view your interface.

5

5
Even when you have the cross-platform color management issue nailed down, don't forget that different platforms present graphics in different ways. This affects how they are seen, and again must be prepared for.

6 | 7 | 8
The colors in this image have transferred perfectly from desktop computer (6) to a Palm handheld (7). But, as you can see (8), the image can't be viewed all in one go.

6

7

8

63

TYPOGRAPHY

Everything is a graphic, including text. To fully appreciate this, look at a foreign-language publication. First you will notice the unfamiliar characters, then you will become aware of the fonts. Now look at a language that's totally alien to you, such as Japanese. The characters will take on a life of their own.

Typography is the art of using the shape of text characters as a graphic, but strictly communicative, art form. Another way to look at it is that text can be

Typography

Typography

Typography

Typography

Typography

Typography

Typography

Typography

M o t

1
Bold text occupies more width than plain text; italicized fonts don't always do quite what you expect. Compare these samples of the font Times. Normal and Italic occupy a similar amount of horizontal space, but Bold is quite different from Bold Italic.

2
Your choice of font will have an impact on space, in particular how much text you can cram on-screen at any one time. Here's how wildly the character widths impact on space for Times, Arial, and Courier—all three are standard fonts for traditional Web sites.

3
Designers have to be aware of "ascenders" and "descenders," the strokes that rise above and fall below the bodies of certain characters. These strokes, and the body heights too, change in size (not just style) with each font and thus affect the legibility of the script.

4
Think about character widths and how they affect the font, spacing, and the words themselves. Some characters occupy considerably more horizontal space than others, and this will have an effect on the amount of text you can fit onto the screen.

Skateboarding is decriminalised

A skateboarder on a halfpipe yesterday

Lorem ipsum dolor sit amet, consectetaur adipisicing elit, sed do eiusmod tempor incididunt ut labore et dolore magna aliqua. Ut enim ad minim veniam, quis nostrud exercitation ullamco laboris nisi ut aliquip ex ea commodo consequat. Duis aute irure dolor in reprehenderit in voluptate velit esse cillum dolore eu fugiat nulla pariatur. Excepteur sint occaecat cupidatat non proident, sunt in culpa qui officia deserunt mollit anim id est laborum Et harumd und lookum like Greek to me, dereud facilis est er expedit distinct. Nam liber te conscient to factor tum poen legum odioque civiuda.

employed graphically in situations in which pictures alone may falter. It's not the opposite of the adage, "a picture's worth a thousand words," but rather an extension of it. A picture that also happens to be text is twice as meaningful.

On the small screens of computer interfaces, you have to be concise with your use of typographical tricks, but they can work wonders. For example, a large initial capital letter at the beginning of a story tells the viewer where to start reading. Bold text immediately tells the viewer which text is more important than the rest. Colored or underlined text might indicate links to other pages or pop-up dialogues. And, even if you don't have the luxury of space to run huge, screaming headlines, you can make them stand out by reserving a particular, thick font for them alone.

To put it another way, good typography can be useful as much for signposting and navigation in an interface as for the simple presentation of factual information. Not least, the style of the text and the way it is presented can suggest an idea or mood, which is something that commercial logo designers use to their advantage every day.

6

Quick brown fox
Quick brown fox

Quick brown fox
Quick brown fox

Quick brown fox
Quick brown fox

Quick brown fox
Quick brown fox

Quick brown fox
Quick brown fox

Quick brown fox
Quick brown fox

65

5
Use font styling to determine your layout structure. By altering the size and style of text, you introduce a set of simple signposts for the viewer. People should know instinctively which text is supposed to be a heading, a picture caption, body text, and so on.

6
Text printed on paper can be reproduced at a resolution of well over 2,500 dots per inch. Text on a computer screen is typically around 72 to 96 dots per inch, or less on certain handheld devices. As you drop the type size on-screen, legibility is going to suffer, and you will therefore need to be all the more careful about your choice of font.

LEGIBILITY

Having recommended that you look at text as a graphic element, you probably now need to be pulled back from the brink of self-destruction! Remember that typography is a way of adding extra meaning to text by presenting it in a graphical fashion. It is not supposed to mean the replacement of original meaning with a picture that looks like a fonted character.

Some interfaces are purely image-based. However, most incorporate at least some text that will be read. Content-heavy Web sites present relatively long tracts of text in a page-by-page article style. People find several short columns ranged across a page easier to read than a single column of text scrolling downward. On the other hand, multiple narrow columns, in which some lines are occupied by only one or two words, are not inviting.

A common legibility example occurs where a button link is reinforced with a text label. The skilled designer might be able to avoid such doubling up, but it's common practice in interfaces targeted at the general

3
Yellow on blue was an on-screen combination that computer programmers discovered early on and employed extensively in the first color PCs. It's a good choice for highlighted panels, although it is probably a bit overused.

1
There's a reason why books are printed with black text over white paper. Nothing is easier to read and the system transfers well onto a computer screen, as shown here.

2
White on black is a stark alternative. The advantage on-screen is that a black background is easier on the eyes. However, the mood of your interface changes completely, which is often undesirable.

4
Now we're having difficulties. Green and orange? Most viewers say this combination flashes in front of their eyes, and the small text is virtually illegible on-screen.

5
Running text over a background image or wallpaper obviously presents its own problem: which color do you make the text if the background color isn't constant? And, even if the text is legible, the viewer might be so distracted by the image that the text goes unnoticed.

ou read me? can you read,RGB)

d me?

read me?

6

ZDNet ▼   🎁📋A' ← 6 ▼

The order, issued by the U.S Court of Appeals for the District of Columbia Circuit, means that the government can resu-me proceedings before a federal district judge while the Supreme Court decides whether

7

ZDNet ▼   🎁📋A' ← 6 ▼

The order, issued by the U.S Court of Appeals for the District of Columbia Circuit, means that the government can resume procee-dings before a federal district judge while the Supreme Court decides whether to take Microsoft's request for appeal.

The mandate returning the case to the trial court will be issued seven days from Friday, the order states.

8

Home   Domestic flights   Foreign flights   Help   Contact

9

6 | 7

PCs and Macs aren't the only platforms that support custom resizing of text, as this palmtop screen demonstrates. Make sure that your interface accommodates such typographical tinkering by the viewer.

8 | 9

These two treatments of a row of buttons force your eyes to look in different places. Where the buttons are identical, you're forced to read the text. Where the buttons are iconic, you tend to look at them first to find a meaning before trying to read their text labels.

public to make everything as clear as possible. But when you employ this technique, ask yourself if the text label works in harmony with the button. Is it obvious that the text goes with a particular button? Does the font match the style of the button? Is it obvious to the viewer whether to click on the button or the text, or both?

You need to make it clear which elements are high in the visual hierarchy so that the viewer knows which text to read first. Is one link more important than another, even though the button graphics are identical? Are pieces of text being cropped off because you have emulated the wrong screen size?

CROSS-PLATFORM TYPE

Typography is a powerful tool and fonts are your friends. But you may not be given the freedom to do much with either, depending on the platform on which your interface is designed to run. Unless you are delivering an interface complete with the hardware, such as within a booth, there can be too many loose ends to make design-led typography a guaranteed hit.

A Web site or distributed presentation may end up being viewed on a computing platform that is different from the one that you used to create it. Quite apart from all the usual cross-platform issues (layout, browser support, color), there's no knowing which fonts are available to the viewer. Even if you restrict yourself to using default Web browser fonts, some of your viewers may have uninstalled them. Others may be running platform-specific Web browsers or multimedia players that never had those fonts to start with. One way to overcome this is to stick with a browser's default font set, which means that you lose control over layout precision. Another approach is to turn important fonted text (logos, headlines, flashes, and so on) into image files. Another still is to make use of a plug-in player that

1 | 2
Here's the same HTML page as seen in identically sized screens on a Mac (1) and a PC (2), both using the Internet Explorer browser. Although mostly the same, the two versions differ in the way the text flows. And yet both platforms provide supposedly the same fonts: Times and Arial.

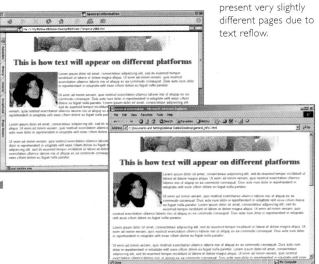

3 | 4
A common solution to the above problem is to set very specific table areas for the text to flow in. However, all this really solves is the reflow problem when a viewer changes the size of her browser window. Here again, the two platforms present very slightly different pages due to text reflow.

5
Most infuriating of all, of course, is that the original page in your Web design package looked like neither of these anyway. Learn to always preview your pages across platforms before going live with them.

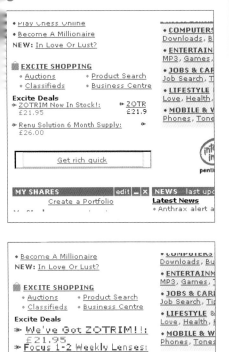

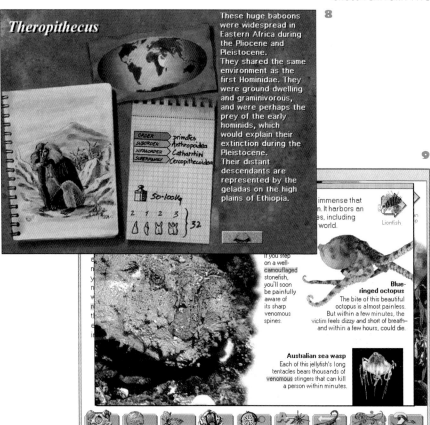

6 | 7
It's not just different platforms that can sometimes cause font trouble. Here you can see an isolated font rendering problem on a Web page under Internet Explorer (6), yet it's perfectly okay under Netscape (7). Both were run on a Mac.

supports embedded fonts, such as Acrobat PDF and certain self-running presentation packages. However, all these precautions will be swept aside if something other than a mainstream desktop environment is being used. An interface destined for a Palm OS-based palmtop, for example, will offer marginally fewer fonting options than one prepared for the PocketPC platform. If you are creating an interface that is supposed to be completely cross-platform, such as a Web site, you should try to find out for yourself what happens when your pages are viewed on a palmtop.

Ultimately, you should prepare separate interfaces for the different platforms. You may have to reprocess pages for general Web access, palmtop presentation in AvantGo and MobiPocket formats, and possibly also a low-graphic or text-only version.

8 | 9
Right from the early days of multimedia development, designers came up with a fail-safe solution to font unpredictability across platforms: embed the text into the presentation as if it is a graphic. The text you see here can't be highlighted, copied, or searched, but it looks exactly how the designer intended it to. For all the everyday advantages of HTML, graphic text remains a much more reliable approach when screen layout precision is essential.

OTHER VISUAL CLUES

This chapter has avoided concentrating on the creation of pictures and the other general issues of graphic design. Such issues are related to content rather than to the interface. But there are other kinds of graphic elements that can be used to good effect.

For example, consider incorporating images within standard dialogue boxes and pop-up messages. You will often find this device used within software applications, such as when a large red exclamation point symbol tells you that a dialogue is a warning or is very important. "What dialogue is not important?" I hear you ask. Good question, but in practice there are always dialogues and messages that can be casually dismissed by the viewer, while others indicate that a critical command needs their immediate attention. Don't overuse such a device, or the viewer will grow accustomed to the warning symbol and end up casually dismissing even the most critical messages.

1 | 2 | 3 | 4 | 5 | 6

Portal sites such as Yahoo need to put across a lot of information, and certainly a lot of links, within one page. But as this breakout demonstrates, it's not necessary to put everything in boxes or to insert rules between each section in order to establish independent areas within that page. Some panels here, a rule there, and just enough white space between the sections should be enough by way of visual clues. Adding extra divisional elements would simply crowd the page even further.

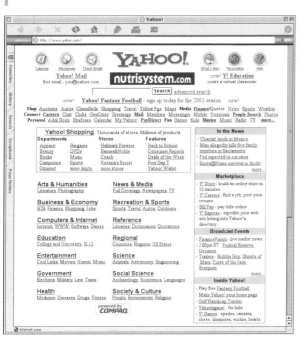

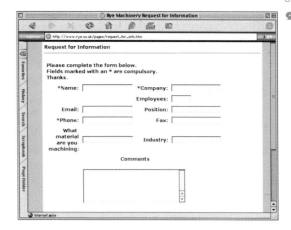

Another example, found in many form pages on Web sites these days, is the "essential field" marker. Let's say you are prompting the viewer to enter personal details such as his or her name, address, and so on. To present a friendly impression, speed up the interaction, and possibly also to conform to data protection laws, you can indicate which fields can be left blank by putting markers next to those that have to be completed. Just be careful with your use of color here: red is usually seen as a warning, so lots of red text or asterisks might give viewers the impression that they've done something wrong.

Other graphic devices that might be helpful (or could become a hindrance if overused) include those borrowed straight from print design, such as horizontal rules for separating stories or areas of a page on the screen. Going to the multimedia extreme, animation actions can be visual clues in their own right, attracting attention to particular items or giving a tactile impression that an icon or thumbnail is a "clickable" button rather than just a tiny picture.

9 | 10 | 11

Simple highlights can assist simple tasks. Here are a few examples in which interface designers have marked up certain items of content to be distinguished from others. The color approach probably works better than the plain asterisks, but maybe not so well if your viewer is accessing your interface with a black-and-white screen such as a palmtop.

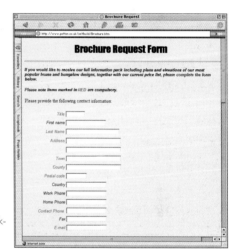

7 | 8

If you have control, or at least some say, over the way dialogue boxes and other pop-ups appear in your interface, try to phrase them helpfully rather than the usual robotic "syntax error" or useless "there was a problem" messages. Also, consider using pop-ups for important information when you need to push it in front of other events on-screen.

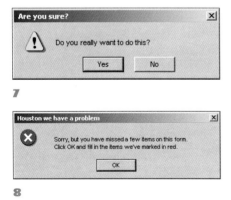

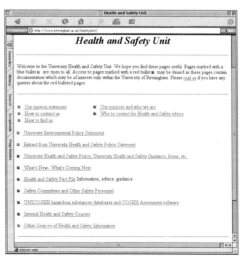

71

ROGUE'S GALLERY

1

2
Actually, this isn't a bad layout at all because it perfectly suits the subject matter of clip art and icons with its kitsch look. But be warned that too many densely packed graphics can render your interface less readable by those with even moderate sight difficulties. Remember, the amount of light that passes through the eye of a 60-year-old is only one third of that passing through the eye of a 20-year-old.

3

4

1
This is the classic "cheap" look borne by a million home pages created in guest bedrooms around the world. Unfortunately, this one is actually for a professional image marketing company.

3 | 4
In the Showcase section at the back of this book *(see pages 124–177),* we've covered some original and clever ways of using HTML support within modern email packages. Right here, though, you can see for yourself a couple of superbly appalling examples of how not to do it. The first (3) looks oppressively drab, while the second (4) is almost unreadable.

5

The look of this email subscription newsletter may be boxy and symmetrical, but that's a graphic design issue for you to make your own judgment on. Our concern is that all the boxes and panels in this very long newsletter are really quite a challenge for the average e-mail package to format. Some packages actually run out of memory while attempting to do so.

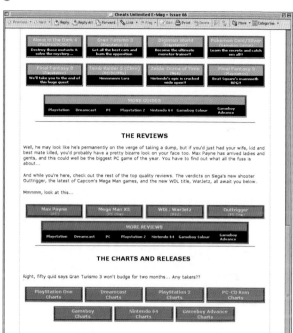

6

This multimedia title is offered on a hybrid CD format designed for PCs and Macs. When the CD is opened on a Mac, the viewer is faced with a massive file and folder listing that scrolls down ten screenfuls. Maybe the first game is "hunt the program." Never forget, your interface begins the moment the viewer inserts your disk, visits your site, or downloads your presentation.

7

Now we're running the program, and it's actually a lot of fun once you get the hang of it. But what are you supposed to make of this central navigation graphic when you first arrive? Try to guess what the icons in the colored areas mean (there are no pop-up hints). The only recognizable one is the maze game in the center; the rest are arcane or plain misleading. The blue section shown here that has the mouse pointer over it looks like an exit-door symbol, but in fact it takes you onto some cartoons. If you want to exit, you have to click on the green Power button instead.

7

TRIGGERS AND LAUNCHERS • 84

INTEGRATION: MULTIPLE WINDOWS • 86

INTEGRATION: MULTIPLE PROGRAMS • 88

CLOSING THE LOOP • 90

ESCAPING THE LOOP • 92

ROGUE'S GALLERY • 94

CONCEPTS OF NAVIGATION

It's not human nature to stay put for long. If it were, the entire race would still be clustered around what is now central Africa. Maybe our DNA is programmed to seek change, momentum, and advancement, or maybe we just have a low boredom threshold. Certainly all of these factors are evident when you see how people browse computer interfaces.

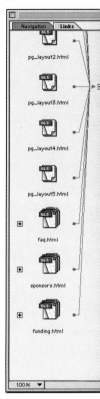

3

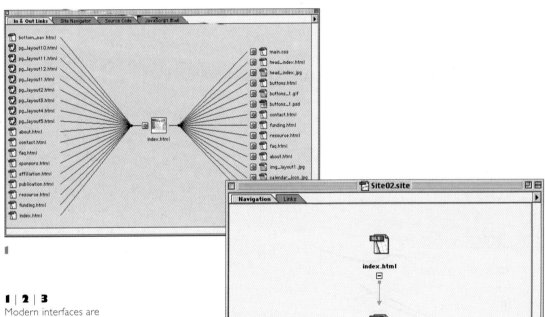

1

1 | 2 | 3
Modern interfaces are usually page-based in one form or another. But these "pages" aren't always read one after another in succession. Mapping out a hierarchical or looping collection of interrelated pages can be quite a task, so it's just as well that the software you use to create them can handle the structure too. These three maps are actually different views on the same Web site within Adobe GoLive.

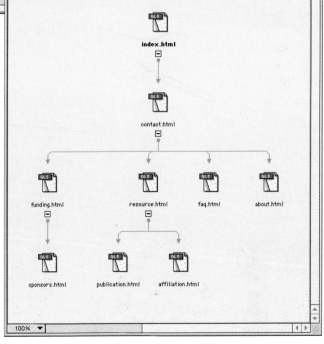

2

4
As you'll find out in this chapter, it's not enough that your presentation has a well designed structure: the interface should explain the structure to your viewers. In order to get anywhere, a traveler needs to see some signs.

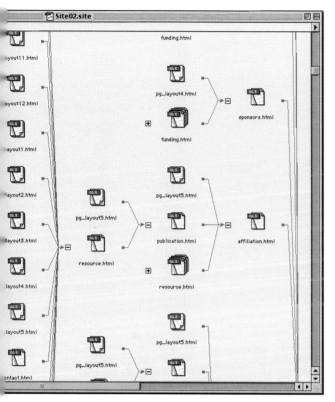

The fact that an interface needs direction ought to go without saying. But consider how the term "navigation" is interpreted in two very different ways in the traditional seafaring fashion. For some, it means a series of signs that lead you on to your intended destination, like a set of coastline landmarks. For others, it means nothing more than a guide that tells you where you are in relation to where you were and therefore isn't intended to lead you in any particular direction.

A good interface needs to meet both of these expectations. Some people just want to be taken from A to B. Others want to go to C via Q and might be prepared to leave the alphabet altogether. Perhaps most interesting are those who thought they knew where they wanted to go, realized they were wrong, and were willing to be led to somewhere better. Without straining this analogy too far, it's the equivalent of Columbus hunting for India and discovering America instead.

So navigation in an interface needs to do more than just lead on to the next screen. Good navigation needs to tell you where you are, remind you where you were, and offer recommendations of where to go next. If viewers make a mistake, good navigation will allow them to go back, or even to start all over again from the beginning. It ought to be possible to exit the interface in order to go on to another, and then to continue later from where they left off within the first one without having to start all over again from the beginning.

Ultimately, navigation should do more than offer a method of changing what's on-screen. It should also put the viewer at ease. As soon as people feel as though they are trapped inside a sealed place, they'll grasp at any opportunity to break out. If your stylized, cutting-edge interface leaves casual visitors feeling like outsiders, they'll just move on to the next one.

Trickiest of all, your interface must sit comfortably alongside everyone else's. This chapter investigates how navigation can help or hinder an interface, and also provides some sound principles for practical design.

77

VISUAL SIGNPOSTING

There's no getting away from it, computers are visual devices. We like to pretend that there's an element of multimedia in there, too, but audio is definitely the poor cousin. Most people could happily use their computer without any speakers, but it would be impossible for them if the monitor was switched off.

Not only is an interface presented visually, it also relies upon visual methods to establish the very rules of navigation. In the future, voice recognition technology may well supplant our current reliance on visual links and buttons. Even so, there will always be situations where this won't be appropriate, such as in booths within noisy shopping malls and—for those who haven't tried it yet— voice-operated mobile phone dialing when standing next to a busy road. Until these issues are solved, people will always scour interfaces for visual clues.

As we saw in the previous chapter, graphic design dictates the mood of an interface, states its intention, identifies itself as a coherent unit, and reinforces the message (or product/service) it was created to promote. All of these factors extend to links and buttons, which are the very nuts and bolts of digital navigation. But there is more to it than just keeping arrow buttons to a color scheme or graphic theme. They also have to be located in a place where people will know where to find them, and be presented in such a way that different types of navigation buttons are easily identifiable.

Think in terms of road signs: they are usually positioned at the side of a road or sometimes overhead because you should never have to swerve your head around to try to discover where they are. Expressway

1
Compton's 3D World Atlas Deluxe isn't as button crazy as some other encyclopedic products, and everything is well ordered. The navigation controls are arranged neatly along the bottom, and there's a scrolling country list on the right-hand side.

2
The children's educational series "Oscar The Balloonist" always features a simplistic set of icons across the bottom of the screen, built into a ladder graphic.

2

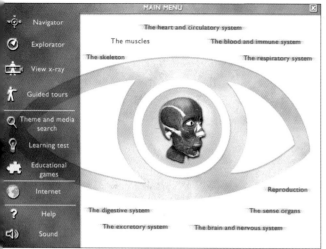

signs usually follow a particular color, main highways are indicated with another, and every now and then you'll pass a sign that tells you exactly where you are.

Reflecting such principles back onto interface design, I'm sure we all agree that it's boring and predictable that navigation buttons tend to appear along the edge of a window, most often across the top or left. However, that's where people expect to find them, so that's where they'll look first. Although your artistic temperament might be crying out to try something new, it is best to keep to accepted visual clues, such as the classic play-stop-pause-rewind buttons that have been borrowed from tape recorders. If you do depart from the familiar, make sure that you have a good reason for doing so and are not just doing it for your own amusement.

3
Interactive Human Body opens with a main menu screen that is simply a collection of buttons. But notice how the main controls are listed in a panel on the left, while content categories are scattered around the main screen area.

4

4
Amazon opts for the most common approach to Web site design, presenting a row of sections across the top and an additional list (worded slightly differently) down the left.

5
Apple's own Web site incorporates the same section tab concept as Amazon, but adds a second row of sub-sections in a colored bar underneath. Be warned, however, that not everyone notices this second row.

PROGRESSIVE BROWSING

Some people read a newspaper in strict order, starting with the masthead at the front and reading right through to the sports pages at the back. Others prefer to dip in here and there, and perhaps return later to sections or stories that they had initially skipped. In either case, one thing remains constant: the newspaper itself has been printed in a progressive page order. If the pages were numbered out of order, and the sections split up randomly, the newspaper would be difficult for anyone to navigate, no matter which way they preferred to read it. In other words, it's the underlying progressive sequence of pages that makes non-sequential navigation—dipping in and out—possible.

This principle is worth remembering when you are building an interface that is made up of individual screenfuls. Although the Web explosion suggests that people have learned to surf interfaces by jumping directly to pages that interest them, they will still want to know where to find the information that they've skipped. And other people will want to plod through and read everything systematically.

Getting the right balance can be difficult depending upon the computing environment of your interface. PowerPoint presentations, for example, are intended as progressive slide shows, so you'll need to work harder to ensure that navigation tools are available that will let viewers skip ten slides ahead without having to tap the arrow key ten times. Web sites, on the other hand, are merely a collection of individual HTML pages; your Web design software might handle inter-page navigation automatically, but it's up to you to decide if and how a progressive page order should be established.

▌
Another legacy of the Web explosion is the adoption of the forward/back paging concept. The idea is to make it easy for viewers to retrace their steps if their page skipping has led them down a dead end. The only problem is that it introduces a potentially confusing duality between progressive and non-sequential browsing. Does a button labeled "Previous" take you back to the previous page in the progressive order, or to the last page you viewed? Your interface must make the distinction clear.

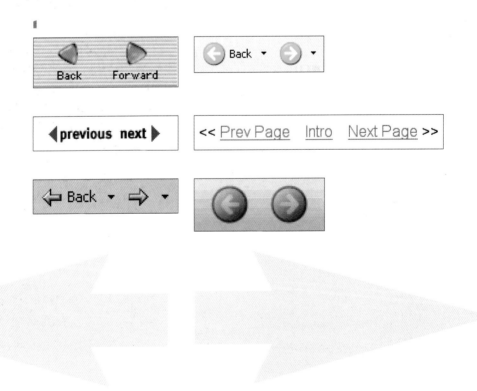

2 | 3

t is often assumed that PowerPoint trots along in page order, but you can very easily build buttons into the pages that either reinforce that order or let viewers quickly jump to a home page. It's just a matter of adding Action buttons and customizing where they point to. You'd also be advised to improve the amateurish design of the default buttons themselves.

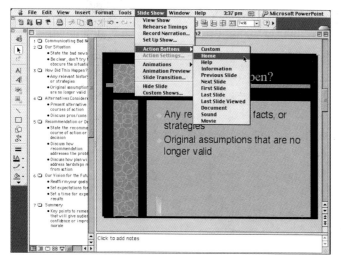

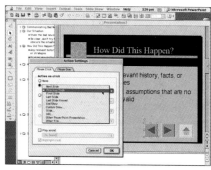

4 | 5

As with PowerPoint, Acrobat documents can be enhanced with buttons and bookmarks to help viewers navigate. For example, you might use Acrobat to turn a list of contents into a jump list. As well as being able to animate the buttons a little, with Acrobat you can set the link to go to a particular part of a page at a particular zoom level.

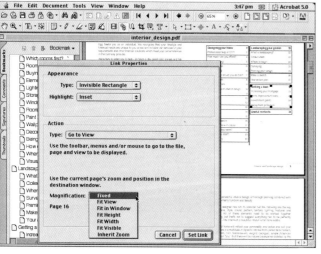

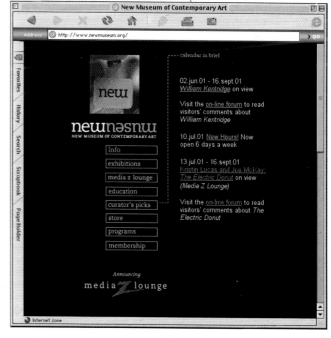

6

See how this Web home page for the New Museum of Contemporary Art in New York presents a very simple array of sections to explore, each marked in a little green rectangle. This is not just a random selection of things to see, but a list of pages to visit given in the most appropriate order that they should be visited in.

HYPERLINKS

Hyperlinking is the action of jumping to another place within an interface, typically by clicking on an active link button, part of a picture, or specially tagged text. The place that is being jumped to can be located in the same screen or page, another page in the same document, or indeed somewhere in another document entirely. Hyperlinking was invented to add functionality to large digital documents such as Help files and operations manuals, in order to let people jump straight to the places that interest them in a non-linear fashion rather than forcing them to scroll through progressively.

Standard hyperlinks appear as text that is highlighted in some way, in order to suggest that it will act as a link when selected. Traditionally, a text hyperlink is underlined, but you don't need to stick to this rule as long as your interface makes clear what is a link. To reinforce the suggestion, Web browsers and presentation software usually transform the cursor from an arrow to a pointing finger when hovering over a link, so make sure that any custom interface you're working on does something similar. Be careful about this, though, when creating cursor sets. If you are designing a shoe store's presentation interface and decide to replace the pointing finger with a slipper, it could be considered witty, but will be totally unhelpful to the user.

Hyperlinks can be built into any graphic object these days. You can even build multiple links into a single image by setting up an image map using any mainstream graphics package. Just make sure that the invisible map borders

overlay appropriate areas of the image accurately, and that the image itself makes it clear where the hyperlinks lead to. Carving up the black and white patches on a picture of a cow into an image map is meaningless, for example, unless perhaps you've employed JavaScript rollovers *(see page 102)* to pop up link labels as well.

Some links can be automated or time-delayed. For example, you might set up a link so that it activates immediately at the end of an animated intro sequence, which means that your viewer won't be standing around waiting for something to happen. Likewise, you can time-delay the page links to turn any interface into a self-running slide show, or to jump to a Help window if a viewer spends too long on a certain page.

The core function of hyperlinks can end up being more of a curse than a blessing if you aren't careful: they may kick viewers off one location and take them to another, possibly one they didn't want to go to. Later in this chapter, we'll tackle the issue of linking back and stopping viewers from getting lost.

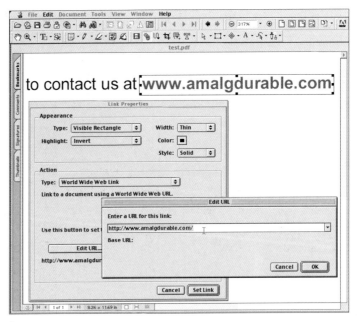

It's not just Web pages these days that employ HTML links. You can build Web hyperlinks into just about any presentation and animation package, including Acrobat (as shown here). The hyperlink can direct the viewer to a site on the Internet, a local network, or perhaps an HTML-based virtual site on the CD that you have distributed the presentation on.

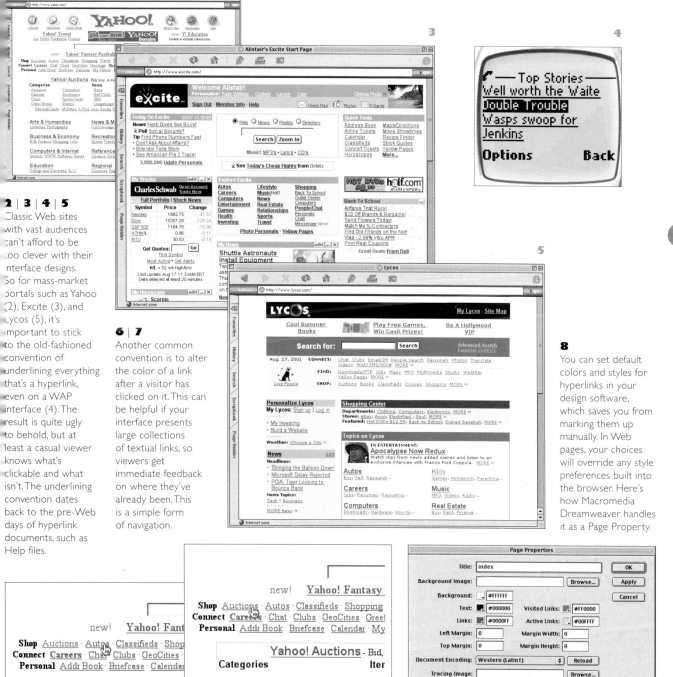

2 | 3 | 4 | 5

Classic Web sites with vast audiences can't afford to be too clever with their interface designs. So for mass-market portals such as Yahoo (2), Excite (3), and Lycos (5), it's important to stick to the old-fashioned convention of underlining everything that's a hyperlink, even on a WAP interface (4). The result is quite ugly to behold, but at least a casual viewer knows what's clickable and what isn't. The underlining convention dates back to the pre-Web days of hyperlink documents, such as Help files.

6 | 7

Another common convention is to alter the color of a link after a visitor has clicked on it. This can be helpful if your interface presents large collections of textual links, so viewers get immediate feedback on where they've already been. This is a simple form of navigation.

8

You can set default colors and styles for hyperlinks in your design software, which saves you from marking them up manually. In Web pages, your choices will override any style preferences built into the browser. Here's how Macromedia Dreamweaver handles it as a Page Property.

TRIGGERS AND LAUNCHERS

Links can do more than jump to another place. A link has the ability to make things happen in an interface, making it interactive rather than just a browsable electronic document. If you are designing an interface using a multimedia-authoring package, you can script buttons to do anything. If you are working on less ambitious projects, you need to remember that links can be used as triggers for other events, or to launch other programs. This is true for Acrobat PDF documents, presentation slide shows, and Flash-enhanced Web sites. Pointing a link to a multimedia file should launch the required player with the file loaded.

It's possible with Web design software, as well as graphics presentation packages, to turn a link into an interactive trigger. For example, you might tag a "Print" button to start printing the on-screen window as soon as it is clicked, or set it up to prompt the viewer with a Print dialogue. If your interface includes a form that you want the viewer to complete, you may need triggers to bring up Help windows as required, as well as one to collect and probably encrypt the form data before saving it somewhere or sending it back to an on-line server.

For Web pages, many of these triggers and pop-up messages will need scripting with HTML, JavaScript, or Flash. But other types of interface design software might make it easier. Building simple interactive programs with a moderately customizable interface is very straightforward with modern database applications such as FileMaker and Microsoft Access. Pop-up messages such as "Are you sure?" can help to keep form data consistent. You may also find it quite untaxing to adjust the interface of mainstream Windows programs using Visual Basic for Applications (VBA), although that is programming territory. Sometimes a trigger need only hint at interaction. A button labeled "Click here to see an animation" will make the process feel more interactive than it would if the animation ran automatically.

84

1
One of the limitations of Web browsers is that you can never be quite sure how a printout will appear. But you can prepare an alternative page layout for printing purposes only. Note how this Internet bank has provided a "Print" button under the statement.

2
Having clicked the "Print" button, the viewer gets the chance to customize the statement period and appearance. Notice that a "Preview" button is now available.

3
This preview indicates how the printout will appear. The viewer can now click on "Print" for a formatted hard copy of the statement without the navigation menus appearing down the left.

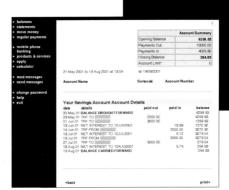

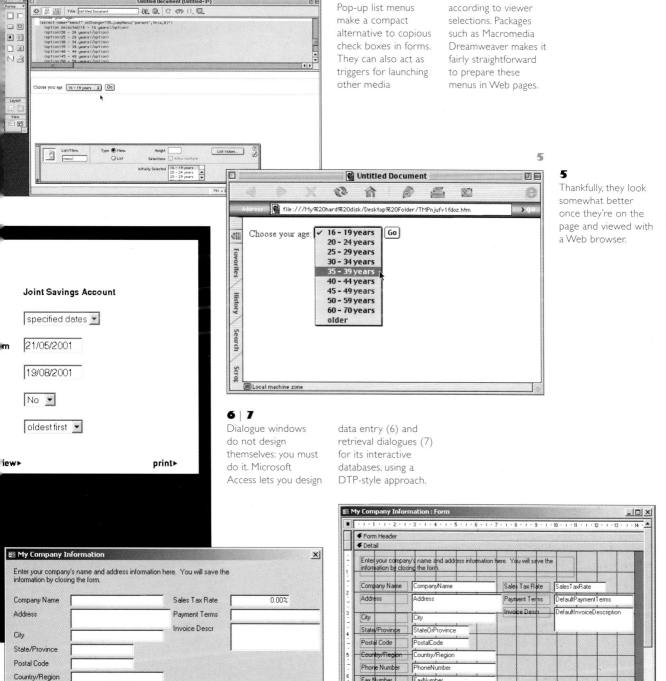

4

Pop-up list menus make a compact alternative to copious check boxes in forms. They can also act as triggers for launching other media according to viewer selections. Packages such as Macromedia Dreamweaver makes it fairly straightforward to prepare these menus in Web pages.

5

Thankfully, they look somewhat better once they're on the page and viewed with a Web browser.

85

6 | 7

Dialogue windows do not design themselves: you must do it. Microsoft Access lets you design data entry (6) and retrieval dialogues (7) for its interactive databases, using a DTP-style approach.

6

7

INTEGRATION: MULTIPLE WINDOWS

Computer environments always include a mixture of blessings and curses. For example, single-window interfaces such as WAP phones and booth units make things easy in some respects because they deal with only one screen at a time. The only problem is that the user experience is made up of a sequential plodding from one screen to the next—there is no escape from that.

Working with a multiple-window interface allows two or more pages to be available for immediate access. But it can be easy for people to get confused when faced with a disjointed screen arrangement like this. New windows hide old windows, so it may not be long before the viewer has forgotten how to get back.

If the environment for which you're writing an interface supports multiple windows, keep this in mind. Make sure that navigation buttons are provided clearly in every window. If necessary, and if the system supports it, break the window into panels or frames so that the interface presents multiple views simultaneously, without the cumbersome overload of multiple windows. However, you should be aware that some people bear an irrational grudge against frames in Web pages!

One feature that's definitely worth using in a Web-based presentation is the opening of off-site links in new windows. By putting external pages in a separate window, you avoid kicking viewers out of your own interface and instead let them navigate the two sites independently. Stand-alone multimedia titles can also make use of a multi-windowed approach by keeping the core navigation tools available in a central window and putting the actual content in another. This works nicely for CD-based encyclopedias, for example. And, while it might look seamless and cool to integrate Internet browsing right into your CD-based title, it usually makes more sense to go on-line in a separate window. That way, the viewer can close the Web window when they want.

1 | 2 | 3

Anyone with a Web browser can choose to open links in new windows. If you have prepared a presentation that is supposed to follow a strict sequence, make sure that the viewer knows which page or slide is which. The tutorials on Adobe's Web site are spread over several pages, but each page bears numbers and step numbers that can help viewers find their way back from a multi-window mess. They would be easier to use if the names within the title bars were also numbered.

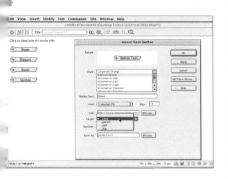

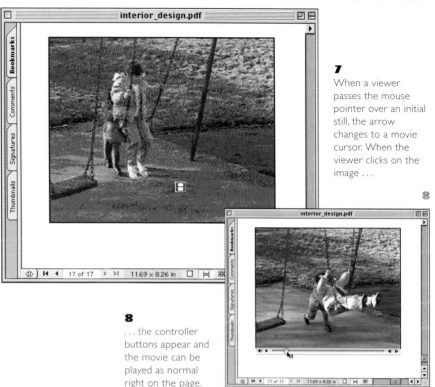

7

When a viewer passes the mouse pointer over an initial still, the arrow changes to a movie cursor. When the viewer clicks on the image . . .

8

4

Web design software such as Macromedia Dreamweaver allows you to link to "blank." This ensures a link opens up in a new browser window, which is a good idea if you are pointing to pages off your site.

8

. . . the controller buttons appear and the movie can be played as normal right on the page.

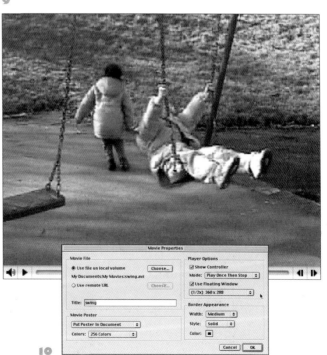

9 | 10

Now when the viewer clicks on the embedded movie still (9), the movie itself opens up in its own window in the center of the screen, but with the same minimalist controller. The advantage of this approach is that the movie becomes the center of attention rather than being lost somewhere on a page. It also vanishes when it's done, returning the viewer back to where they were beforehand (9). Alternatively, you may prefer to force the movie to run in an independent floating window (10).

5 | 6

When putting a movie into a presentation, the usual approach is to embed the movie directly and include some playback controller buttons.

INTEGRATION: MULTIPLE PROGRAMS

Unless you are authoring a stand-alone multimedia title that has everything built in, you may find it useful to incorporate links that fire up external programs to handle different kinds of data. The obvious example is linking to QuickTime video files or to MP3 audio, which then gets played back outside your presentation interface. This can be risky, however, if the presentation is being distributed. Links to external programs assume that the viewer has already installed them. Consider the number of times that you have browsed the Web and come across an error saying that you don't have a required program, plug-in, or the right version of a plug-in. That will happen unless you have complete control over the device handling your interface program. It's not just Web browsers that are affected: the same goes for PowerPoint presentations and other proprietary slide show programs, triggers within Flash movies, etc.

In your favor is the fact that free playback utilities such as QuickTime, Real Player, and Windows Media Player support multiple competing formats, so just one of them should be enough. When distributing your content on CD, you should consider including the relevant player installer on the disc, too, to get around this problem. This will need to be licensed, of course.

Don't restrict the function to multimedia. If you know the software that is installed on a viewer's computer, you can link to all sorts of document formats. Linking to RTF or TXT files will launch whatever word processor is on the machine, for example, which saves you from having to prepare a scrolling text dialogue.

Finally, weigh the pros and cons of embedding external player panes into your interface or letting them launch into independent floating windows. Beginners prefer the former, and it's also more suitable for small screens and booth applications. However, power users prefer the latter, and this option also protects your presentation from some performance glitches.

88

1
It's bad enough when viewers don't have the right program to run something. Here, the viewer has the right program, but the Web browser doesn't know whether to use it. Nor will the viewer.

2
In this example, at least the interface designer tells the viewer in advance which external utility programs are required, and he or she has also provided a link to the correct

download page. The trick in this sort of situation is to explain everything in advance, in as much detail as possible, rather than leaving it all to chance and error messages.

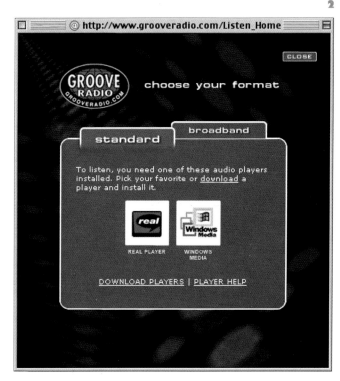

3

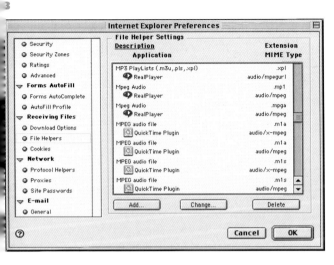

4

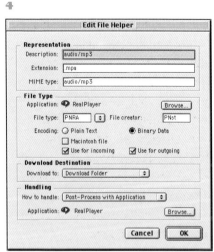

3

When setting up a machine for booth use, ensure that all the required programs are installed and recognized. Web-based presentations rely on installed "helper" applications.

4

A "helper" application will have added itself to the browser's list when it was installed. If not, you'll have to edit the details.

5

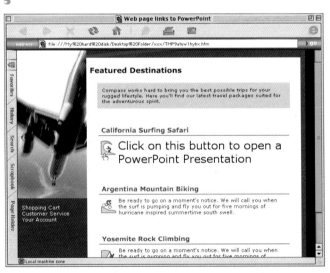

6

5

Don't restrict yourself to multimedia files when you are building interfaces that link to external programs. Here, for example, we've set up a Flash button on an HTML page to launch a PowerPoint presentation.

6

If PowerPoint has been installed, the program will start and open the document. You can get the presentation to load up in full-screen self-running mode. There is a Word thumbnail on this slide.

7

Clicking on the thumbnail launches Microsoft Word with the linked document open, ready for reading or editing. You can, of course, embed an icon link into this document that links back to the original Web page.

7

CLOSING THE LOOP

An interface must present its content as an identifiable whole. But no end of visual design tricks and color coding will maintain this self-contained identity if the viewer keeps falling out of it.

Falling out can be a common problem with slide shows and Web sites that run on people's own computers, but it's just as serious in dedicated devices such as e-books, digital satellite receivers, and those little LCD menus on laser printers. When people lose their way on a single-window dedicated device, they often take the drastic measure of switching the machine off and then back on again. This might do the trick, but it's hardly the hallmark of a good interface, and can even be highly destructive if the device in question is an expensive touchscreen point-of-sale machine.

Let's retrace the golden rules of navigation:
• Navigation buttons should be available to the user in every view.
• Make it clear where viewers currently are, not just where they've been or where they should go next.
• Allow viewers to go back to a previous screen, page, or menu in case they made a mistake.
• Make it extremely clear how to get back.
• Provide a single button to jump right back to the start ("home") in every view.
• Let viewers jump to principal categories or sub-sections quickly.

The idea behind closing the loop is to round off potential dead ends, but you need to think like your audience to understand what constitutes a dead end. Having followed a sequence of links and ended up on a page they didn't want, your viewers will want to go back, skip to a more likely section, or start from a higher level in the page or menu hierarchy. The page they arrived at might be packed with links, but if these don't refer to familiar or relevant topics, or don't provide a return to the start, viewers will see it as a dead end.

If you are a Web content designer, you have to deal with two sets of navigation buttons: one in your interface and another in the browser's own interface. Forward and Back arrow buttons on your pages will be expected to do the same thing as the browser's Forward and Back buttons. If they don't, you've broken the loop.

Further care is required when using frames. If implemented casually, the main content window in a framed site will never register in the browser's URL (Uniform Resource Locator) line. So, when viewers hit the browser's Back button instead of your own page navigation buttons, they will get thrown off your site.

▪
As computer-based concepts filter through to the public, you can assume an awareness of hierarchies. Viewers no longer expect information to be in strict sequential order: thanks to audio CDs, MP3s, and general computer usage, people are used to non-linear structures. However, you can choose how to present this hierarchy. The most common is the progressive browsing model, in which you start with a welcome page and fork out to other pages.

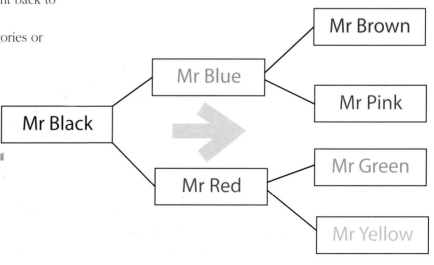

4

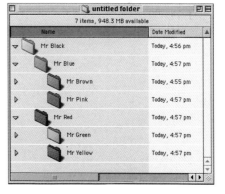

4

Most computer users are accustomed to one way of representing hierarchical information—the folder tree. This structure is top-down and left-right.

2

Yet the same information can be represented using a classic top-down hierarchy. This makes the use of Forward and Back buttons a confusing instead of helpful element to your interface.

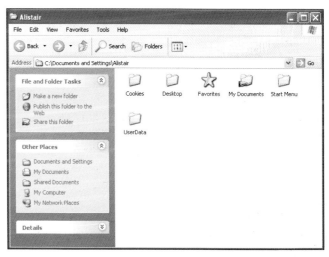

5

2

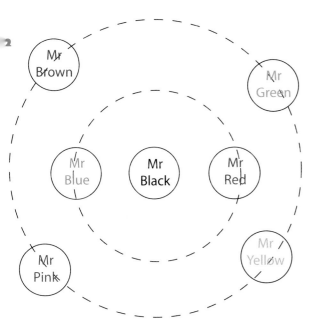

3

In reality, your interface is probably sitting in front of a structure that looks like this. It spreads out in concentric rounds or layers, but it may be possible to leap directly from any one layer to another in one direct step, without navigating the hierarchy.

5

Windows XP and its immediate predecessors employ an interesting approach, combining Forward and Back buttons, which don't necessarily respect a hierarchical structure, with a third "go back up one level" button, which does. For operating systems at least, this "go up" action is much more useful than a "Home" button would be in the same place.

3

```
                    Mr Black
                   /        \
              Mr Blue      Mr Red
             /      \      /     \
        Mr Brown  Mr Pink  Mr Green  Mr Yellow
```

ESCAPING THE LOOP

Make sure that you don't take things too far in your zeal to close the loop—it's a loop, not a hermetically sealed plastic bag. At some point your viewers will want to leave your interface to do something else, so think about what will happen then.

So far, closing the loop has been all about getting people back on track if they got lost. But what if they're not lost? Maybe they have reached the place they wanted to get to and that's it. If printer users have found the command they were hunting for in the LCD menus and have selected it, they will now want to print some files. Do they have to reset the menu manually before the printer goes back on-line? Is this easy to do? Do they even know that they are expected to do it at all?

A similar example can be seen in many WAP browsers. Why is it that the Exit command always seems to be farthest away in the scrolling menus? Why can you never cancel a link to a site that isn't working? It's no wonder that vast numbers of WAP users decide to turn

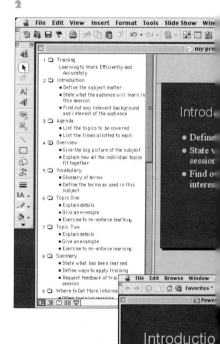

2
You tap the Escape key on your keyboard, that's what. And this is the result. Now consider the number of computer users who have PowerPoint installed (because Office came free with the machine) but have never used it. You don't really want to dump them in the middle of the PowerPoint editing interface.

1
We've seen this problem countless times. Someone has sent you a PowerPoint presentation that's designed to kick in at full-screen, just like a projected slide show in a theater. But you need to check your e-mail or run another program halfway through viewing it. What do you do?

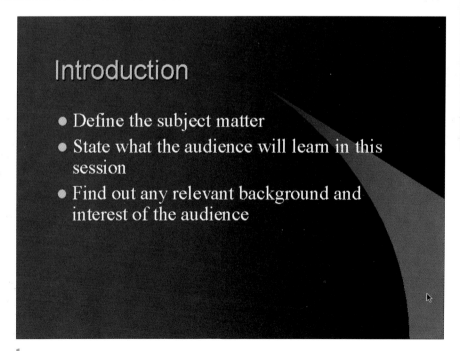

3

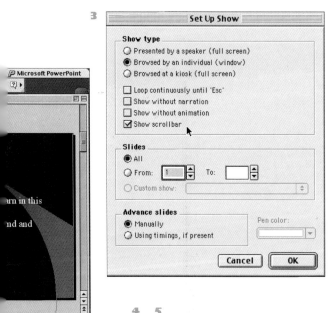

3
To fix this, in the Set Up Show dialogue, change the Show Type to "Browsed by an individual" and include a scroll bar for moving from one slide to the next.

their phones off and on again to avoid this problem. Consider a multimedia presentation or Web site that has been designed to be immersive by running in full-screen mode and disabling the Esc key; some viewers may want to leave the program and do something else. Because of the nature of your interface, they can only exit completely. All the viewers wanted was a temporary exit, but you have forced them to close down. Booths, point-of-sale programs, and other touch-screen systems

93

in public places are very tricky; people tend to walk off and leave the interface midway through. You must ensure that it's clear to the next customer what the situation is, and how they can locate the welcome screen.

4 5

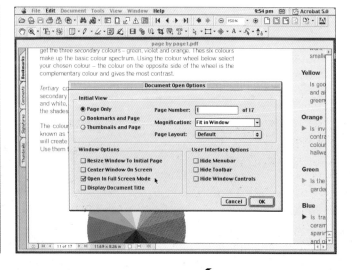

4
Now when your viewers run the presentation, it appears in its own window. They can run other programs without quitting. You are crediting your audience with enough intelligence to know what a scroll bar is. They will truly appreciate this.

5
As with PowerPoint, avoid setting up any self-contained document to open in full screen mode—unless it's a genuine booth, of course. Some programs such as Acrobat even let you toggle the menu bar, tool bar, and window controls to "off." All of a sudden,

your user will find that his computer's interface disappears when your show starts. This is a great way of frustrating people, and will ensure viewers exit the presentation long before they reach the end—even if they have to restart the computer to do it.

6
This HandSpring Visor Deluxe, like most handheld computers, demonstrates the art of escape. The small screen prevents multi-windowing, but screen buttons and real buttons allow the user to jump to another program with a single tap. Can your interface do that?

6

ROGUE'S GALLERY

1

Connect.
Print.
Copy.
 Forget.

You've seen the ad...

Now find out more

3

WELCOME

Enter the site

16 COLOR™

click to enter

WELCOME TO
OLYMPIC MUSEUM LAUSANNE
HISTORY OF THE GAMES
> français

1 | 2
Having got as far as
persuading potential
customers to visit
your Web site, why
would you then
immediately prevent
them from gaining
access to it? Many
computer users find
"Click to enter"
annoying. Having
typed the URL into
the Web browser,
what else did the
designer think they
wanted to do?

3
Here's the same
problem—but with a
difference. Here,
there is a reason for
halting the visitor at
the first page, since it
acts as a splash
screen to establish
what the site is all
about. But this screen
should only stay on-
screen for just a few
seconds before
switching
automatically to the
real front page.

4
The splash screen
approach is used here
once again, but
unfortunately there
isn't even a "Click to
enter" instruction.
Maybe it's lower on
the page? No, you
actually have to click
on the picture.

2

4

94

5

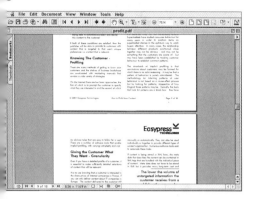

7

8

5

There's a navigation issue in Adobe Acrobat that causes much confusion among less experienced computer users. PDF documents scroll up and down here, but the Next Page and Last Page buttons in the tool bar point to the left and right, as do the Back and Forward buttons next to them.

6

6

All credit to Enter.net for attempting to present a busy and feature-packed portal page on the Web, but where do you start? Navigation, remember, must be easy within a page itself as well as when moving from one page to another within a site.

7

When creating Web pages based on frames, make sure that the framesets are labeled correctly and reflect the content of the main pane. Here is a classic example of a site on which it has been done wrongly, because when you click on the link to Page 2 …

8

… you arrive at Page 2, but the frameset still thinks it's Page 1, as is shown in the window title bar. If you tried to bookmark this page, it would link to Page 1 instead. This isn't an issue with Web browser frames so much as poorly prepared framesets.

SIMPLE ANIMATION: GIF · 98

SIMPLE ANIMATION: HTML · 100

SIMPLE ANIMATION: JAVASCRIPT · 102

ADVANCED ANIMATION: FLASH · 104

ADVANCED ANIMATION: FLASH II · 106

ADVANCED ANIMATION: DIRECTOR/SHOCKWAVE · 108

PLAYBACK MOVIES · 110

PANORAMAS · 112

INTERACTIVE MOVIES · 114

3D VIEWERS · 116

3D VIRTUAL WORLDS · 118

3D INTERFACES · 120

ROGUE'S GALLERY · 122

96

SIMPLE ANIMATION: GIF

We have already explored how the use of particular imagery can force people to look one way or another, or how it can be used to depict the logical hierarchy of your presentation. Another way of attracting attention is to make some of the images move. The easiest option to do this with is an animated GIF.

Along with JPEG (the most common image file format), GIF (Graphic Image Format) is the core graphics format for Web pages. But, unlike JPEG, a GIF can store multiple images in one file and flip automatically from one to the next. Animated GIFs can play back in many presentation packages, such as PowerPoint as well as Web browsers.

Anyone with some experience in creating Web sites will already be familiar with the limitations of the GIF format. You are restricted to 256 colors or fewer, which makes a GIF inappropriate for photo images and gradients, and the compression is only really successful for flat-color graphics, anyway (such as cartoons, screenshots, buttons, banners, and so on). This applies to both single-image and animated GIFs alike, so you need to think about file size and loading times. On-line or not, large animated GIFs aren't the fastest graphics to

load up on-screen, and anything that delays your interface from operating swiftly is just going to make people think it doesn't work properly. The most common use for animated GIFs is to attract the viewer's attention to a particular thing. In a presentation, it might illustrate an important point. In an educational program, it could highlight a particular menu item. On a Web site, it might draw attention to something that's new or changed since the last time a customer visited. Obviously this arrangement will work best when there's only one animation on-screen at a time—otherwise the viewer will get confused.

As with any graphic, you should use animated GIFs with a purpose. Animated navigation buttons can sometimes help to remind the viewer that there's more to read on the page, if, for example, you employ some moving arrows across the bottom of a screen. But if you're not careful, a simple animation, such as blinking HTML text, can end up looking cheap and cheesy.

Cartoons are by far the most common animated GIF on the Web. The best examples are those with good timing and plenty of squashy, bouncy movement. Keep asking yourself if there's a valid reason for putting an animated cartoon character on the page before you do, though, as there are plenty around that don't serve much purpose.

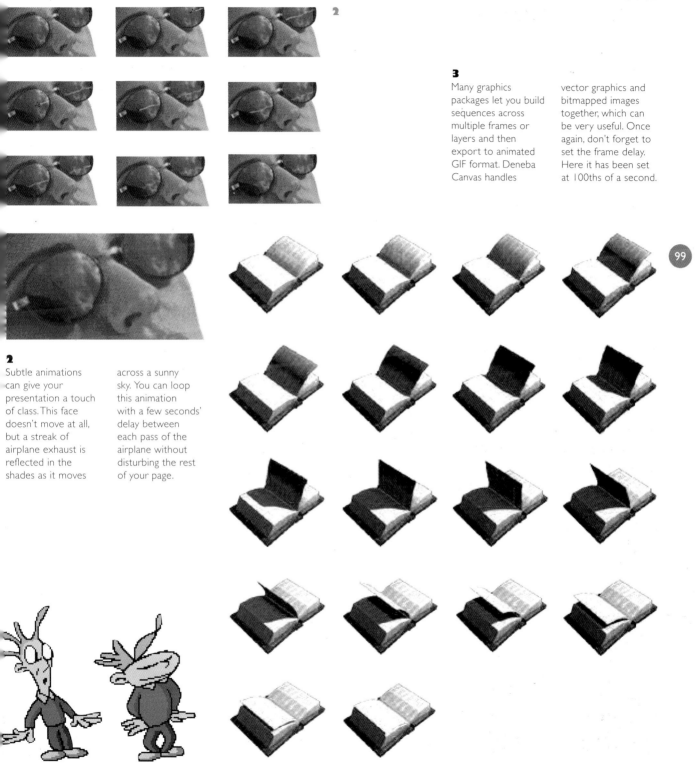

2

3

Many graphics packages let you build sequences across multiple frames or layers and then export to animated GIF format. Deneba Canvas handles vector graphics and bitmapped images together, which can be very useful. Once again, don't forget to set the frame delay. Here it has been set at 100ths of a second.

2

Subtle animations can give your presentation a touch of class. This face doesn't move at all, but a streak of airplane exhaust is reflected in the shades as it moves across a sunny sky. You can loop this animation with a few seconds' delay between each pass of the airplane without disturbing the rest of your page.

3

SIMPLE ANIMATION: HTML

The Hypertext Markup Language, HTML, is the language of the Web. Since its inception, it has undergone constant revision, but you should never lose sight of what HTML was created for originally. Basically, it's a system for presenting text that contains clickable links to other bits of text. Support for graphics, let alone animation, is almost incidental.

The people who develop Web browsers often try to embellish dull old HTML with proprietary tricks. One of the earliest "tricks" to be developed was blinking text: just put a BLINK tag around some text and watch it flash on and off in your Web browser. This usually looks awful and is poorly supported by modern Web browsers, so you'd be better off using color or size for emphasis rather than blinking—or perhaps you could create the text as a more controllable animated GIF.

Another embellishment is the scrolling marquee, which sends a line of text scrolling horizontally across a Web page in ticker-tape fashion. This might be a good

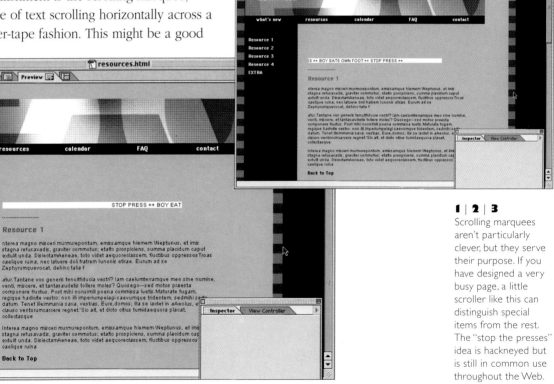

1 | 2 | 3
Scrolling marquees aren't particularly clever, but they serve their purpose. If you have designed a very busy page, a little scroller like this can distinguish special items from the rest. The "stop the presses" idea is hackneyed but is still in common use throughout the Web.

4

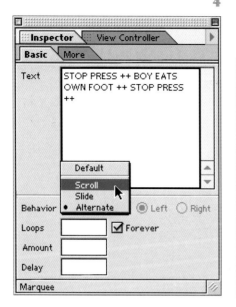

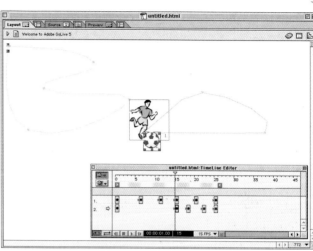

Setting up scrolling marquees is easy these days. In Adobe GoLive, which is shown here, you just type your text into a box, choose a scrolling type, and then customize the timings.

101

6

way of attracting attention to a "stop the presses" item, but is otherwise limited as an interface function simply because text that moves is difficult to read. The other problem is that such extensions are specific to Web browsers, so a feature supported in one browser probably won't work in any other.

Version 4 of HTML, which is supported by all of the modern browsers, incorporates "cascading style sheets" (CSS) that may be used for formatting text and layout. One of Version 4's features involves the concept of dynamic layers, which makes it possible to overlap text and graphics. Objects on these layers can also be given a motion path. This means that you can produce smooth path-based animation on a Web page similarly to how you would in a conventional multimedia presentation. This can be a stylish alternative to blinking messages or animated GIFs, but be warned that objects moving over the top of text are highly irritating to viewers if they are trying to read the text.

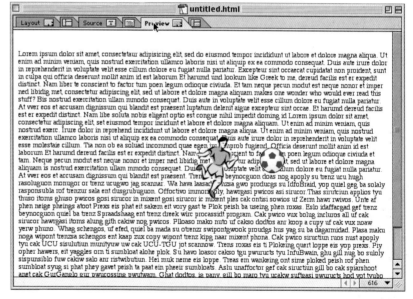

5
Dynamic HTML (DHTML) layers let you add objects to an HTML page that can then be placed or moved over the top without disturbing the background. Most Web design programs provide a timeline approach to setting up the animation. You can add more objects and make them appear to interact, such as this zigzagging soccer player kicking the ball.

6
Just to prove the point, we've pasted a load of text into the HTML page to show how the DHTML objects are free to dance around on top.

SIMPLE ANIMATION: JAVASCRIPT

Those with programming knowledge can create their own interfaces from scratch using Java. If you don't consider yourself to be much of a programmer, then consider using JavaScript instead. JavaScript is entirely supported within modern Web browsers, and, as the name suggests, it is a scripting language that embeds Java-like objects within an HTML page. Examples of this include drop-down lists, contextual menus, and other such user-triggered routines that can make a Web-based interface look a lot more interesting.

You can hire a programmer to write the code for all this, but these days you can pick up ready-made JavaScript morsels from all over the place. Many are provided free within Web-centric graphics packages, while the intrepid designer can always pinch JavaScript from other people's Web sites by copying and pasting the code from a browser's Source window. Beware of copyright issues, though: many scripts include a copyright statement that may allow copying as long as you preserve the author's credit and the copyright statement itself. Others may forbid copying outright.

It's easier to stick with the JavaScripts that are provided with graphics packages because you generally don't have to worry about the code, just its application. The most popular of these is the so-called "JavaScript rollover," in which a link button changes color or shape when you move the mouse pointer over it and again when you click on it. This is often effective for evoking a tactile feel within a flat interface. The button might light up when your mouse moves over it, for example, and then appear to press inward when it is clicked.

Take care: rollovers can be overdone. Put too many on a screen, and they'll respond with a clumsy delay that confuses your audience. Also, because each rollover "state" is a unique graphic, you're increasing the file size of the whole page—an important consideration if this is going on a Web page that will be accessed on-line.

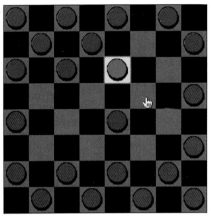

1 | 2
This interactive checkers board (1) and the Rock, Scissors, Paper game (2) are nothing more than JavaScripts running in a Web browser. You could just as easily present a calendar showing today's date, present random pictures, let viewers change the background color, and so on.

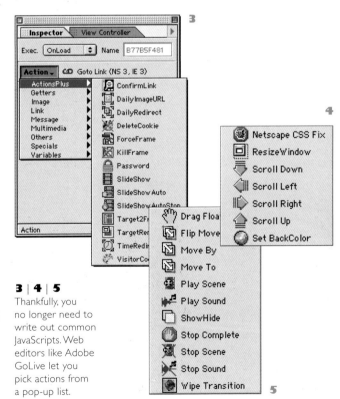

3 | 4 | 5
Thankfully, you no longer need to write out common JavaScripts. Web editors like Adobe GoLive let you pick actions from a pop-up list.

6

The flexibility of JavaScript is such that you can assign regular triggers to not-so-regular actions. For example, you can cause Web links to trigger when the mouse passes over a button rather than when the button is clicked.

7

JavaScript rollovers change the state of images—typically buttons or slices—in response to mouse actions. Passing the mouse over this red Stop button changes it to a green Go, while clicking on it causes it to brighten and letting go of the mouse button turns it purple. By using rollovers, your viewers will get a clear visual response as they navigate the interface.

8

You can overdesign on/off buttons, of course, but with careful use and a little imagination, they can do the talking for you, providing a tactile feel but also keeping your interface "clean."

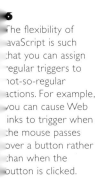

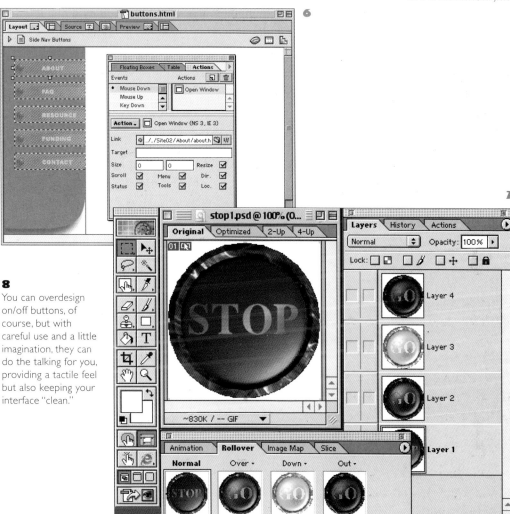

103

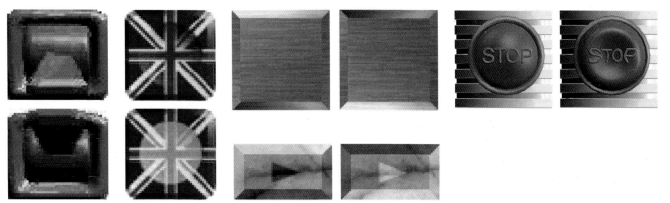

8

ADVANCED ANIMATION: FLASH

Frustration with HTML and Java as platforms for sophisticated on-line interfaces and animations led to the development of Macromedia's Flash. Flash arose from a project concerning fast-drawing vector graphics, which subsequently expanded to include a plug-in module to let viewers see the graphics in a Web browser. By the time Macromedia had bought the technology and hired its creator, Jon Gay, Flash was being used for vector-based animations on the Web.

The core strengths of Flash, then, are due to the fact that vector graphics make smaller files than bitmap graphics and will resize themselves to fit any screen without going jaggy or pixellated. And while an animated GIF is a sequence of bitmaps, a vector animation need be nothing more than a single image with altered points. This means that Flash animation can often occupy a mere 10 percent of the file size of an equivalent animated GIF, thereby lending itself to on-line use. Being small, it typically runs more smoothly, too.

104

1

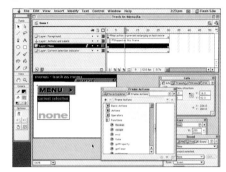

1
Apart from animation, Flash is used to produce custom interface elements, such as this drop-down menu. Things can be scripted manually, but most designers are happy to use ready-made procedures.

2
Here's how that drop-down menu sample appears in Flash Player or a Web browser.

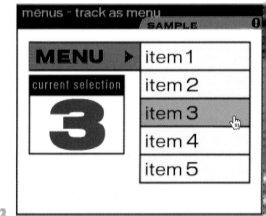

3
Some designers hurdle the HTML/Flash issue by getting the user to choose between them!

4
Here, the Flash version has been chosen. As you move the mouse over the bookends on the right, the relevant color-coded section title is repeated horizontally above the mouse pointer.

For the interface designer, Flash can be approached in different ways. Over the page, we'll examine it in terms of it being an animation system. But, perhaps more importantly, it has also inherited many features from Macromedia's ShockWave technology *(see page 108)* and can therefore support many fundamental interface functions. In fact, many stand-alone multimedia presentations, as well as some of the finest award-winning Web sites, are pure Flash; the only HTML involvement is as an opening page that automatically triggers the Flash "movie."

With Flash, you can design page-based presentations or scripted multimedia actions within a fixed scene. Because you're working within a vector graphics environment, you can focus on the placement of objects, prepare multiple animated objects to react with each other, and completely customize your interface. You can use fonts, colors, and pictures anywhere and in any combination. Keep an eye on the overall file size. Remember that Flash playback is a graphics processing function, so if your viewer has an old computer, your interface will limp along badly.

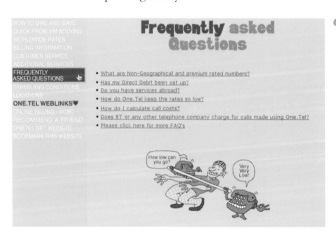

105

5
Click on the bookend you're interested in, and the Flash interface takes you there, via more cartoons and tricks. Note the escape routes to the main contents page and previous/next pages.

6
So you've chosen the HTML-only version. There's less fun stuff to play with, and the text is resolutely horizontal. However, the pages have been brightened up with JavaScript rollovers *(see page 102)* for the section titles on the left.

ADVANCED ANIMATION: FLASH II

Despite the full power of Flash to support user interactivity and effectively take over the entire interface environment, most designers still regard it as an animation file format. This is understandable: Flash's powerful interactive features are script-heavy and take a lot of learning, while Flash animation is extremely simple. In fact, you don't even need a copy of the Flash program to use it, since most big-name illustration packages let you export frame-based sequences to the Flash player (SWF) format as well. There are also a few packages that just offer the dynamic animation features of Flash but leave out the complex interactive features.

The stereotyped impression of Flash is the often cursed "intro screen," a self-important Web site's opening page, which consists of a convoluted animation intended to reinforce company branding. Web sites are usually accessed over a slow modem line, so these Flash intros can take a minute or more to download. Once they start running, people invariably hate them anyway. The sensible designer will incorporate Flash's ability to start running the animation while the file is still downloading; adding a "Skip Intro" button somewhere on the screen is helpful, too, if rather self-defeating. If you must use Flash intros, make sure that they automatically trigger a link to the main HTML page when they've finished. Ending with "Click here to enter site" means that you've introduced an obstacle: the viewer wanted to go to the site in the first place, but you just stopped them with your Flash movie.

Used carefully, Flash can produce surface gloss around an interface. As an alternative to JavaScript, you can employ Flash to improve the presentation of navigation buttons and consistent branding across your interface. And though not essentially an animation feature, Flash's vector base ensures the graphics are resolution-independent. This means that a Flash animation or entire interface, properly produced, will re-size automatically to fit the window in which it is viewed.

106

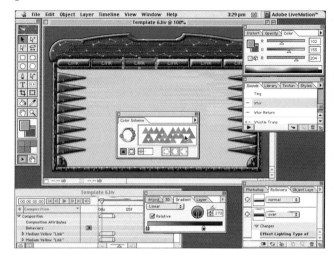

1
Flash isn't the only program around for creating Flash-format "SWF" movies. Adobe's LiveMotion can produce complete interface replacements, but is best employed as an animated Web graphics package.

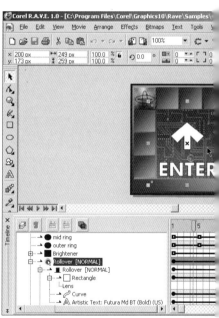

2
RAVE, part of CorelDraw, is another Flash alternative for SWF animation. Most actions are turned on and off with a click in an object-layer timeline.

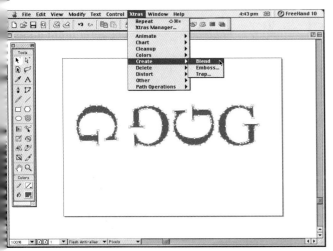

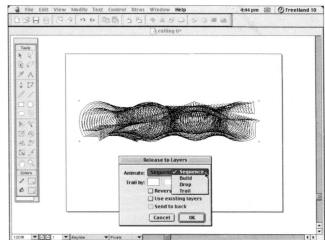

3

Most vector illustration packages can export graphics directly to Flash movies, too. Here in Macromedia FreeHand, four copies of the letter "G" have been rotated across the page. These will act as key frames when generating a blend between them.

4

Displayed in Keyline mode, you can see the effect of the blend: it has generated progressive, intermediate transformation steps. This is the same as "tweening" in an animation package. The steps can now be sent to separate layers.

5

A new layer has been automatically created for each of the blended steps. These will become the frames of the animation sequence.

6

Finally, it's a simple matter of exporting to Flash's SWF format, making specific changes according to the functions the illustration software supports.

ADVANCED ANIMATION: DIRECTOR/SHOCKWAVE

Flash might have a lot more to offer than just animation, but it's hardly the last word in interactivity, either. For the complete interface-building experience, you should consider Macromedia's Director package and the ShockWave format. Director, as every graphic designer will know, is the most popular program around for creating highly sophisticated multimedia presentations, educational titles, and even quite a number of interactive computer games, too. ShockWave is an implementation of this multimedia content, featuring compact file sizes and therefore suiting on-line delivery.

Creating stand-alone programs with Director is not easy. It's a heavyweight application that puts a lot of emphasis on scripting and even sports its own script programming language—Lingo—which you'll need to learn. But if you really want to produce a complete interface, there's no other way.

2

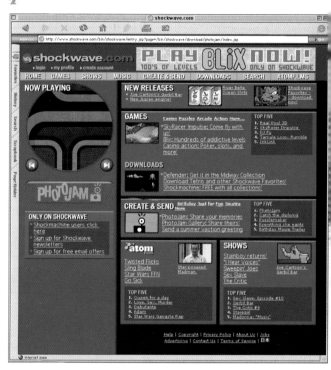

108

1
Macromedia Director began life as a multimedia-authoring package for CD-based titles, but has grown into a Web-enabled ShockWave production studio as well. But it's not all about kids' software and games: here, Director is being used to create interactive training materials with their own built-in animations and interface.

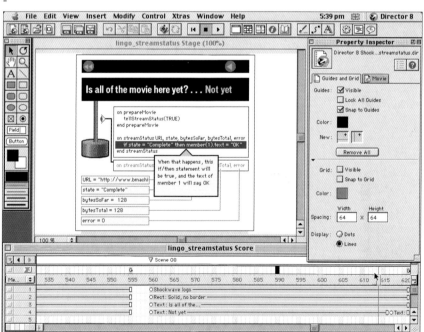

2
One of the first places to check out for ShockWave content is www.shockwave.com. You'll find some of the best examples in the showcase that starts on page 124.

3

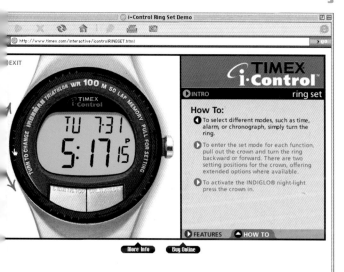

It's this completeness that distinguishes ShockWave from Flash. Although both are optimized for Web presentation, ShockWave breaks beyond mere triggers, animations, and vectors. A ShockWave production is a program in itself, complete with streaming audio and video. It can incorporate Flash as just one element along with many others, such as 3D objects and XML (Extensible Markup Language) data.

You can take advantage of ShockWave in a number of ways. Building multimedia titles is self-evident, but it also allows them to be installed on a Web server and then run remotely and efficiently from a remote computer. This means that you can produce quite complex interfaces without expecting viewers to download everything before the interfaces will play for them. ShockWave is good as an additional feature to existing content, too. You may already have built a presentation in PowerPoint, HTML, or whatever, but clicking on a particular trigger fires up the ShockWave element separately. In this way, ShockWave is not part of your interface, but is used to reinforce branding, add value to your content, and encourage people to return.

3

Director's advanced interactivity functions allow designers to take real-life objects and make them appear to work on-screen. This Timex watch can be operated as a virtual product using a mouse, but it responds in precisely the same way as the real thing does.

4

ShockWave doesn't have to be about games … but you can't ignore that it's a great way of packing on-screen toys into small packages. Here's RealPool repackaged as a free demo, an application that uses ShockWave plus 3D extensions.

4

PLAYBACK MOVIES

Just as pictures and illustrations add a sense of vitality to the printed page, moving pictures somehow enliven the flat-look interface of the computer screen. And in the same way that photographs give more depth to print material than a vector graphic can, video playback transforms on-screen animation from a cartoonish feel to give a "we-mean-business" impression. Video movies have the power to surprise and delight viewers, who still rarely expect more than very basic animations built into presentations and Web sites.

The big drawback is that digital movies make for large files, and this will have a ripple effect on whichever method you use to play them. If your interface runs directly from the computer—for example, if it is a retail booth, video wall, or projector presentation—then the quality of the playback will be dependent on the performance of that computer's processor, graphics card, and audio hardware. If the interface is Web-based or otherwise distributed on-line or across networks, the file size issue is critical.

1

2

3

1 | 2 | 3
When a viewer triggers a movie, there's no knowing what player utility is going to fire up. Often, a person will have several players installed without even knowing it, and each one will vie with the others. Here, the same video is being played by QuickTime (1), Windows Media Player (2), and a free ATI utility (3). The problem is that your viewers might end up with a player interface that they are totally unfamiliar with, or is out of sync with your page designs.

Roundabout video

Use the controls above to play, pause and rewind the movie

Roundabout video

Use the controls above to play, pause and rewind the movie

For these reasons, on-line video movies are often presented as independent objects that open in their own window. This can be useful for the viewer, who then has access to the full set of playback controls as the video is "streamed" across the Internet from your Web server. This works well for the popular RealVideo and QuickTime formats, as many Web users are familiar with the relevant video player software utilities. However, the less experienced computer user won't know what to do with a movie player. Thankfully, you can integrate—literally embed—movie windows into a wide range of interface page formats, from HTML and PowerPoint presentations to Flash, ShockWave, and even Acrobat PDF. In fact, you can actually work backward with the PDF format because its support for embedded QuickTime allows you to trigger Flash movies in turn. The result is a seamless video pane with or without playback controls underneath, all embedded into the interface window. This also avoids a separate playback window getting inadvertently hidden behind something else on-screen.

The trick in getting it right is all to do with the "seamless" aspect. If an embedded movie looks glitchy, doesn't make clear how it should be played and stopped, or takes a while to start playing at all, you need to take a look at the other video formats or even other solutions altogether.

4

One way out of this situation is to embed the movie within your own interface. Doing this is easier than you might think, especially if you are working with Web pages,

PDFs, and PowerPoint presentations. In this instance, we're embedding a QuickTime movie into a plain Web page using Adobe GoLive.

QuickTime 5 Required

Click here to play movie.

5

On the page itself, the movie appears along with basic playback buttons across the bottom. All your movies will present the same buttons no matter what computer they are played back on, as the buttons are embedded into the page.

6

You might want to have the option of this little warning popping up on the page, just to tell the viewer what you've done. The last thing you want to do is

create a glitchy performance, which will make people think your video is actually a rough-looking still image, without any explanation.

PANORAMAS

Videos are OK, but there is a danger that they will turn your viewer into a digital couch potato. If users are just watching things happen, you risk frustrating them.

In some instances in which you might have used a video, an interactive panorama may work better. The most common type of panorama format is QuickTime VR (Virtual Reality). This is basically a super-wide-angle still image that the viewer can explore by panning left, right, up, and down, and by zooming in and out. For example, if you are designing an interface for an estate agent's customer presentation, there's a lot to be said for showing QuickTime VR panoramas of each room in the property for sale instead of providing a plain QuickTime movie walk through. A dynamic photo-browse control in the hands of the viewer will always come across as less cheesy than a relentless through-the-keyhole video.

QuickTime VR files can be created by photographing panoramas with special lenses or, even more easily, by stitching together a sequence of regular digital photos.

2

1

1
A quick visit to IfYouSki.com provides panoramic views of a large number of ski resorts using iPIX. The panorama panels are embedded into the Web pages. The viewer just clicks and drags to pan around the images, or uses the zoom buttons to look more closely at something and then pull back out.

2
A panoramic walk in the woods used to be a fairly typical QuickTime VR example. But the latest versions of QuickTime offer a complete world, including ceiling and floor areas. This is referred to as "cubic" VR technology because it seems as if the viewer is standing within a graphic cube rather than just panning within a cylinder.

112

Many mainstream photo-editing packages, including Corel Photo-Paint and Deneba Canvas, support stitching and QuickTime VR output, although dedicated software solutions exist for the serious panorama designer.

The main alternative to QuickTime VR is iPIX, which is a popular choice for educational and e-commerce Web sites. IPIX is based on taking two "hemisphere" photos from a digital camera with a special lens, which are then composited automatically to produce the initial panorama. Unlike the do-it-yourself approach to QuickTime VR, iPIX must be bought or rented as a complete hardware-software kit. You then pay licensing fees according to the number of images you process and the kind of site you're publishing for.

One thing to remember with both systems, and any other that may arise in the future, is that they need player software in order to run. Typically, they run seamlessly using Web browser plug-ins, and it's good to know that QuickTime now includes extensions to support iPIX, too.

3
This means that you can let your viewers look down to the grass at their feet. …

4
… or up to the sky above their heads.

5
Many mainstream graphics packages support the stitching of individual images into panoramas, but not all will actually export to the QuickTime VR format or a similar one. Here's VR Toolbox's VR Panoworx in action with the basics of professional QTVR building. First collect your individual shots around a 360-degree range …

113

5

6
… then let the program try to link them together. You can adjust each tile manually …

6

7
… before they are blended, ready for customizing with hot spots and compression settings.

INTERACTIVE MOVIES

If videos add depth to a presentation and panoramas provide a certain measure of real-time interactivity, imagine what a combination of both could do for your interface. Over recent years, technologies have been emerging—especially on the Web—for producing immersive interactive video. One such technology is SmoothMove's iMove system, which is based on "spherical video" action panoramas. The system allows viewers to take control of the movement *within* the image, not just around it. It means that you can trigger embedded actions such as movies and animations. The idea is to present the viewer with an interactive alternative that allows the 3D environment to be enhanced and extended with video. IMove supports hot spots for pop-up content and advertisements, which can be extremely useful. Like iPIX, you have to lease or buy the kit to produce iMove content. The technology does, however, support live streamed broadcasts.

Another possibility is BeHere's TotalView. Based on QuickTime, Windows Media, and Real Player formats, TotalView is a 360-degree streaming panoramic video technology. It allows you to see a complete single-viewpoint spherical environment as a full motion video or animation. You can then browse around this enclosed

114

1 | 2
One of iMove's strategies is multi-camera video. This lets viewers watch an event from any of the cameras that you have set up, and they can also skip from one camera to another as desired. The viewers can't, however, control the cameras themselves, of course.

3 | 4 | 5
Certain types of video cannot be easily designed to be fully immersive, such as this basketball game (the players would have to keep avoiding the camera structure). But you can look around you from the sidelines with TotalView, just like a spectator at the actual event. Here, TotalView is operating as a plug-in for the free Real Player utility.

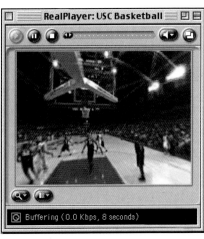

9

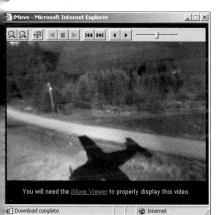

10

6 | 7 | 8 | 9 | 10 | 11
IMove's other approach
is spherical video, an immersive
system that combines live action
with panoramic views. The
example here follows the landing
of a light airplane—the viewer is
free to look around the scenery,
down at the ground, back
toward the tail, and so on
as the video progresses.

11

panoramic video in real time, as if you were in QuickTime VR. It's not entirely immersive, since you're still looking at the scene through a small window, but the effect of the moving images and freedom of panning can be very effective. By putting a camera on the sideline of a football match, for example, you can watch the game, look up at the spectators, or turn around to eavesdrop on the managers in the dugout.

Again, TotalView requires special cameras, lenses, and software before you can start processing the final movies through packages such as Windows Media Encoder or Real Producer. Interactive video can be startling when it is done well, but, as with all video technologies, it is limited by file size and throughput. Viewers need broadband connections to properly run iMove and TotalView.

3D VIEWERS

There's another way to provide an interactive, immersive function in your interface: 3D objects. Instead of giving the impression of standing in the middle of a panorama, 3D gives a model that you can rotate in virtual space while you "walk around it."

Technology for publishing 3D objects on the Web has leaped ahead in recent years. The driving force has been e-commerce, as retail operations demand ways of giving potential customers a more tactile on-line shopping experience. It appears that even if people like to shop on-line, they still end up trudging down to the store to first see the goods for themselves; this is especially true for consumer electronic goods.

Although this is now a hackneyed example, 3D provides browsers with the ability to look around a model of a car that they want to buy. If you can show an accurate 3D model on-line that customers can virtually prod and poke, then you've got a killer e-commerce interface.

Most of the solutions available are provided as export extensions to mainstream 3D-design software such as Alias Wavefront's Maya or Discreet's 3D Studio Max. You create the models and apply the materials, then export them to the relevant viewer format to be embedded into a Web page. Widely used systems include Cult3D, Pulse3D, and ViewPoint. Parallel Graphics' Cortona system, although it still requires a plug-in player, is unusual because it is based on industry standard VRML technology.

3D files in these formats are relatively small: a complex scene may only occupy 100–300Kb.

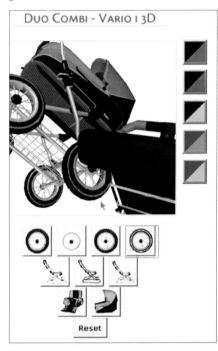

DUO COMBI - VARIO I 3D

Reset

1
Cult3D is an obvious choice for e-commerce interfaces. A viewer can rotate a 3D object in space and can customize its colors, trimmings, etc. Cult3D works for embedded objects in Web pages, Power-Point presentations, and Acrobat PDFs.

2
Cortona uses VRML as the basis of its 3D imaging system. That said, VRML alone couldn't handle all these shiny surfaces, which are supported by the Cortona player proprietary plug-in.

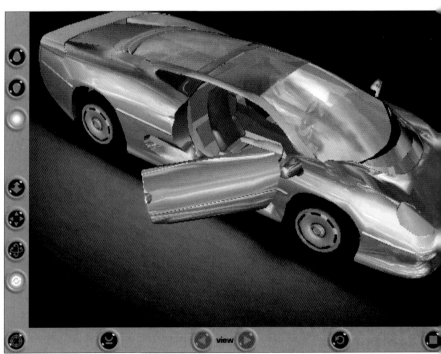

view

116

2

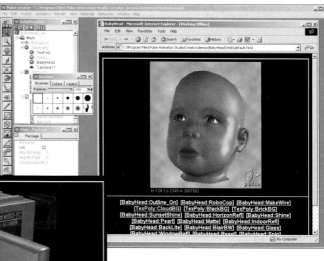

3 | 4

Pulse3D is another 3D player that is popular for training and e-commerce, but it specializes in animated 3D models of people (3) and cartoon characters, complete with audio soundtrack. The Pulse Creator program (4) lets you animate objects that are modeled from your 3D-design package.

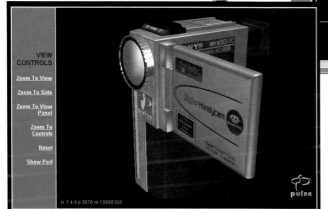

4

5 | 6

Viewpoint technology can be employed for simple presentations of objects that can be rotated in space (6), or for animating complete 3D models. The Aibo robot dog (5) here walks across Sony's Web page while you read about the product.

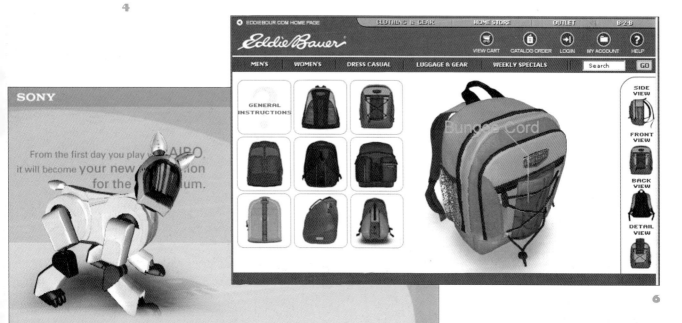

5

6

3D VIRTUAL WORLDS

The common concept of "virtual reality" used to be a complete 3D or cartoon 2D world that you walked around in. After a while, people realized that this was totally dull, so virtual arenas were born, in which multiple computer users could walk around and bump into each other using graphical representations of themselves, known as "avatars."

In the early 1990s, avatars and illusionary 3D worlds were all the rage. Today, interest in virtual chat rooms has diminished. But there's still plenty of room for such 3D worlds in fields beyond entertainment. You might be designing a training package, for example, for which video is a possibility but doesn't quite offer the custom versatility of a 3D environment built into your studio.

Ultimately, 3D virtual worlds are an extension of the 3D viewers concept that was explained on page 116. But instead of designing an object to spin around in space, you're now designing a full-scale 3D scene for panning

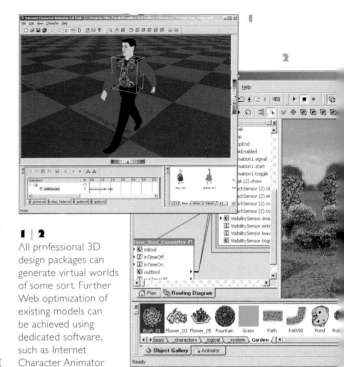

1 | 2

All professional 3D design packages can generate virtual worlds of some sort. Further Web optimization of existing models can be achieved using dedicated software, such as Internet Character Animator (1) and Internet Scene Assembler (2), which are both from Parallel Graphics.

3 | 4 | 5 | 6

Parallel Graphics demonstrates how to pack a big scene into a relatively small amount of data with this VRML reconstruction of Moscow's Red Square. Using the Cortona browser plug-in, it is possible to walk around the square, fly through the entire space, and zoom and pan without restriction. You can see here that the 3D world is very much an illusion: the buildings are merely painted fronts, rather like a Western town in an old cowboy movie.

The 3D data for this Red Square occupies a mere 18Kb, while the graphic resources take up another 373Kb.

3

4

5

118

7

PuppetTime is an authoring program that generates pre-programmed sequences using simplistic 3D scenes and characters. You can't explore things in quite the same way as VRML since the actions and audio track are all scripted, but it allows alternative viewpoints.

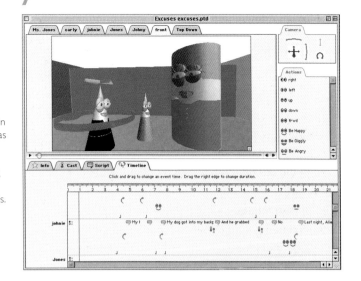

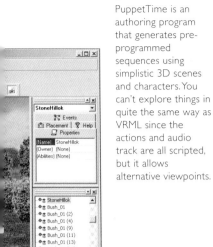

6

around and moving about in—a 3D-model equivalent of panoramas. The handy feature is, of course, that you control what's in the scene because realism doesn't interfere.

Imagine you are working on a commercial interface for a travel company. Let's say that you have included photographs of famous city landmarks and have provided a link to a relevant street map. Now you can also add a simplified 3D model of the city center in which only the landmarks and main streets are shown. The viewer can move around the space, see how close one landmark is to the next, and look behind to see what's on the other side of the street. Clearly, a viewer will obtain a better feel for navigating the real area from a virtual sidewalk than from photographs and maps.

Many standard 3D solutions can be used to export 3D worlds, too, but the VRML-based systems are going to be the best supported for Web sites. And you'd be surprised how compact some of these worlds can be—they rarely reach the 200–300Kb mark.

3D INTERFACES

It's one thing to embed a 3D scene into your interface, but it's quite another to make that virtual world the actual interface itself. Some of the most striking, multimedia-rich Web sites on the Internet are nothing more than HTML shells pointing at full-scale Flash movies. So, following the same reasoning that is behind them, why not fire up a wall-to-wall interactive 3D environment to replace the usual plodding, progressive page-based interface?

You need to have a pretty good reason for doing such a thing, of course. One of the best is the classic "virtual tour," which expands on the virtual world theme but adds more interactive functions. For example, you might be preparing a CD-based educational title or a Web site for a museum. You could stick to the usual encyclopedia approach of searchable categories and topic guides, or you could consider a live 3D walk through of a virtual reconstruction of the museum itself.

120

1 | 2 | 3

The Wellcome Wing of London's Science Museum can be visited remotely over the Internet. Virtual visitors can make their way around the VRML floor and check out the exhibits, which are in the same relative locations as their real-world equivalents. More of the Wellcome Wing on-line exhibition can be found in the Showcase section of this book (see pages 124–177).

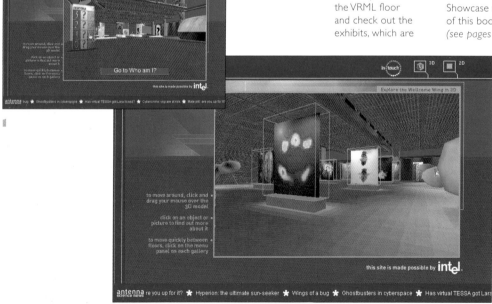

1

2

White Peacock

close window [X]
hi-res version [→]

Special genes control the distribution and survival of cells that add colour to feathers, hair and fur. A variation in these 'white-spotting genes' has made this peacock lose its colour-producing cells and its feathers are therefore white.

Source: Science Museum purchase
Inventory Number: E1999.1117

GM mice
Click thumbnail to enlarge the image in the main window.

3

7

4 | 5 | 6 | 7 | 8
Many individuals have uploaded their multimedia artwork to the Web as virtual portfolios. Here, Avi Rosen has built a complete walk through gallery, complete with an animated floor and ceiling plus live video walls. Images 7 and 8 show the control palettes that are provided for users of the exhibit.

5

8

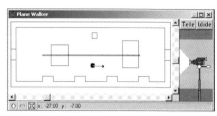

9
The Internet Car Company presents its wares in a 3D-effect site. It's not an actual 3D scene, of course, but the virtual showroom effect combines with the QuickTime VR interior pane to completely replace the normal browser interface.

As viewers move along the aisles, they can click on exhibits to make them pop up for closer inspection, read captions, and operate gadgets.

Clearly, this is a major project that's going to take a lot of time and money to produce. Realistically, clients will only consider it for limited use, such as for well funded sponsored exhibitions or long-duration special events. You could apply the idea in the simplest way possible—a virtual art gallery where you can view the pictures at natural perspective angles, then click on them to get a higher resolution face-on view, for example.

The other main limitation to 3D interfaces like this is that they are perceived as cumbersome when employed inappropriately. In the film *Disclosure*, people had to don virtual reality helmets and gloves, stride down a vast 3D cathedral, and call up an angel to help them riffle through filing cabinets, all in order to open a file. That may be pretty to look at but is obviously crazy, and extremely off-putting to the casual viewer. E-commerce customers accessing a Web site are hardly likely to enter it if the doors alone take five minutes to download. This sort of 3D treatment is good for special events, as a unique 3D interface will make them even more special.

9

ROGUE'S GALLERY

Incorporating animations and 3D into your interface will inevitably make it more complex. Remember that, as far as the viewers are concerned, there's no difference between a simple design and a complex one. They will expect both to work properly, so don't expect any forgiveness if yours doesn't. Here are some issues that crop up time and time again, and so are worth considering now.

1

Viewers open up your presentation, launch your program, or visit your Web site. The first thing they see is a Flash movie, which has kicked in automatically. There's no Skip Intro button, so they assume the movie won't last long and let it carry on.

2

Oh look, the movie is carrying on a bit longer than expected. Viewers start to wonder how to turn the movie off.

3

And so it goes on. Viewers may wonder why the movie is running at all—it doesn't appear to serve any practical purpose.

4

Now the movie has stopped ... or has it just frozen? The viewers are baffled. They try clicking on the screen and discover that the "Welcome" text (in its various languages) is in fact the Skip Intro button. The presentation proper finally starts running, but your viewers are already in a bad mood.

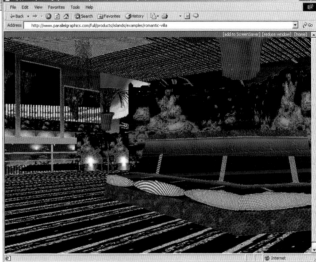

7

One problem with proprietary plug-ins for video and 3D is that they sometimes conflict with a computer's graphic card driver. This scene looks radioactive, but if it's the viewers' first visit, how are they supposed to know that it's wrong?

8

Having changed the number of colors displayed from 256 to thousands (16bit), this is what your viewers will get. Do you think that it is an improvement?

5 | 6

This spectacular example of a cubic QuickTime VR panorama is quite superb. Look at the painting on the wall (5). However, let's take a closer look (6) at it by zooming in and ... oh dear. The moral of the story is not to raise people's expectations too high. You may know there's a limit to the technology, but your audience doesn't: they just think your pictures have "gone funny."

9

Raising the level up again to millions of colors (24bit) has suddenly solved the problem. Maybe you should tell your viewers to do this in the first place.

10

A designer who intends to incorporate Flash, ShockWave, or indeed any other plug-in as part of an interface must build in some checking routines. The program should look for the plug-in and then tell viewers what is required if it's missing. If you leave it to fate, viewers get to see this message instead, which is completely useless no matter which button they click.

11 | 12

Try to be specific about which player utility deals with which kind of multimedia file. If the file associations have been confused on the viewer's computer, you can end up with a situation like this, where the utility tries its best to handle something it can't even recognize.

BOOTHS

O ne of the interface design areas that is least
restricted by conventions and standards is that
of booths and point-of-sale units. Booth information
systems display a healthy willingness to conform to
convention, but on their own terms, by mixing Web
layout methods with their own design ideas and, of
course, sturdy public-access hardware.

1|2

The Vans point-of-sale
booth (1), for example,
can be found in Vans
leisurewear stores in
the U.S., but is firmly
Web-based in its
presentation. In fact, the
booth interface and
Vans's Web site (2) share
the same overall design.

4

3

5

| 4 | 5 | 6 | 7

oser to the Internet
ne is Get2Net, which
a pay-as-you-go
blic access Internet
rvice. Unlike Internet
fés, though, it is
livered to the public
booth fashion, and
e interface includes
stom buttons and
ntrols on a full-screen
eb layout. This lets
wers browse
et2Net content and
f the Web itself from
e same place, in a
gle window, without
tting lost.

6

7

FUTURE DEVICES

Catch a glimpse of what hardware manufacturers have in mind for the next generation of mobile devices. You may soon be designing interfaces and applications for such things. Bear in mind, though, that most of these images are mock-ups or prototypes.

1 | 2 | 3
Nokia looks to be continuing its quest to ban all straight edges from its products with the curvy F4 wireless palmtop (1). Another spin on the same idea, but with a larger screen, is the C5 (2), which purports to be a more Web-like interface. Most conventional of all is the N1 mobile color videophone (3), but note how, even here, the screen occupies over half the unit's space.

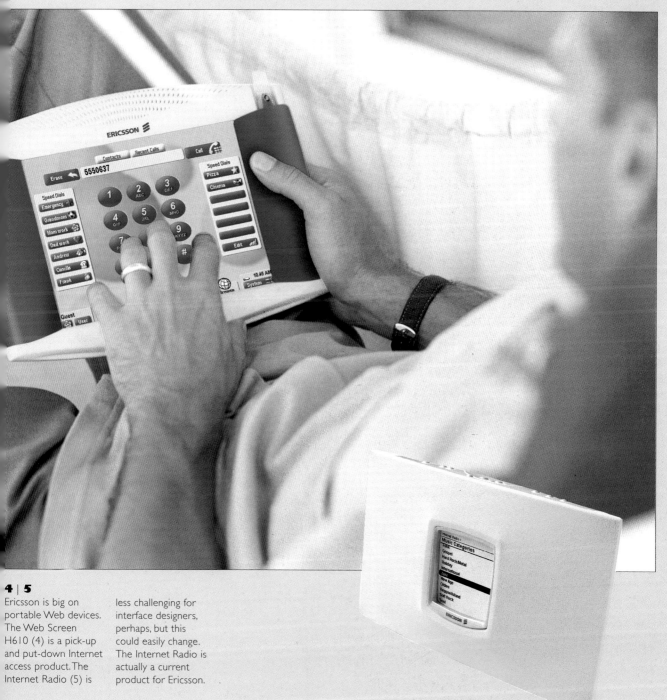

4 | 5

Ericsson is big on portable Web devices. The Web Screen H610 (4) is a pick-up and put-down Internet access product. The Internet Radio (5) is less challenging for interface designers, perhaps, but this could easily change. The Internet Radio is actually a current product for Ericsson.

5

SMALL SCREENS

Portable computing devices prove that a lot of future Internet content will still need to be designed for small screens. Most of the machines that are shown here are designed to be held in one hand when in use and slipped into a pocket when not in use. How do you build an interface for such a small area?

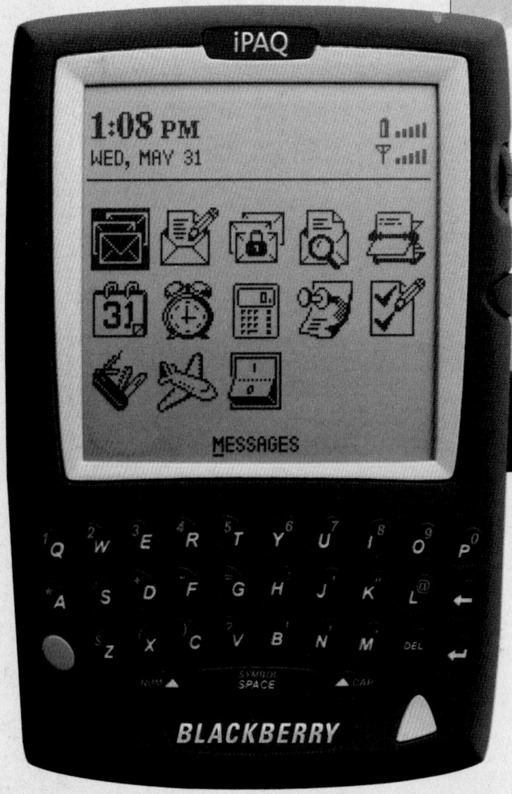

1
From Compaq, here is a new style of palmtop, which has been dubbed the iPAQ Blackberry. It employs an iconic interface on conventional grounds, but the tiny QWERTY keyboard buttons open it up to wider use by people who can't work with a stylus. Previously, the idea of building a keyboard into a handheld device was scorned by many manufacturers. This newly found acceptance could open new doors for interface designers.

2
Compaq has been hard at work developing a new generation of portable computing devices. One of the most striking is its planned Internet Appliance. Take a closer look at the keyboard and you'll get an idea of how small it is. It's built to be carted around the house, placed on a countertop, plonked on a coffee table, etc.

3

Compaq's mainstream line of palmtops runs Microsoft's Pocket PC operating system, which is worthy of showcasing in itself. It manages to maintain the Windows look and feel, especially in color, while at the same time be optimized for a portrait-oriented, compact screen.

4 | 5

The Palm OS interface is special, too, incorporating a permanent so-called "silk-screen" area for command entry with stylus strokes and handwriting recognition in general. HandSpring's Visor Edge (4) shows this quite well. The combination of hardware buttons, silk-screen buttons, and stylus strokes means that you never have to navigate menus or a sequence of links to get where you want to go. HandSpring's Visor Prism (5), which has a wireless unit attached, is a clear reminder of the need to make certain Web sites palmtop-friendly in their small-screen layout.

WAP

Although WAP is generally regarded as a text-based system, there are certain developers who are demonstrating how WML's support of simple graphics can be used in novel ways. Quite apart from the usual site logos and fonted section headings, the images can be built into a more complete WAP experience.

1

2

7

3

4

5

6

1 | 2 | 3 | 4 | 5 | 6 | 7
LudiWap is a slick entertainment site. Here we've chosen to play a LudiWap adventure game. At each step along the way, a brief text excerpt establishes a scenario and prompts you to make a choice. This is accompanied by a relevant graphic that helps to establish the mood or a character. And so you move forward in the adventure step by step. Without the graphics, it would be mildly diverting; with the graphics, it's surprisingly compelling.

8 | 9 | 10

If you want an idea of what WAP could really be like if done properly, take a look at some of the solutions currently being developed by Openwave. These screens come from a new wave of color-screen mobile phones that provide menu-style navigation with minimal scrolling. One element of this is called Download Fun—inevitably, Ringtones are at the top of the list.

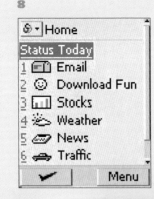

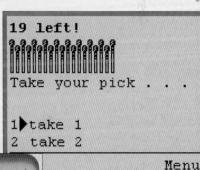

133

11 | 12 | 13
The interface also supports graphic wallpapers—a far cry from phone logos—that can be downloaded into collections.

14 | 15
Similarly, you can download screensavers for your mobile phone, keep several handy, and change the default selection from time to time.

16 | 17 | 18
Here are some more products based on Openwave's phone browser: Openwave's own five-day city weather forecast (17), the Matches puzzle game (18) from One Bad Monkey, and an animated welcome message, designed for early risers, from Animobile (19).

OS REDESIGN

The race is on to produce a new operating system that will live up to the expectations of a fresh millennium. Particular attention is being paid to the user experience of working on a computer. We are now seeing the biggest redesign of GUI since Apple launched the first Macintosh in 1984.

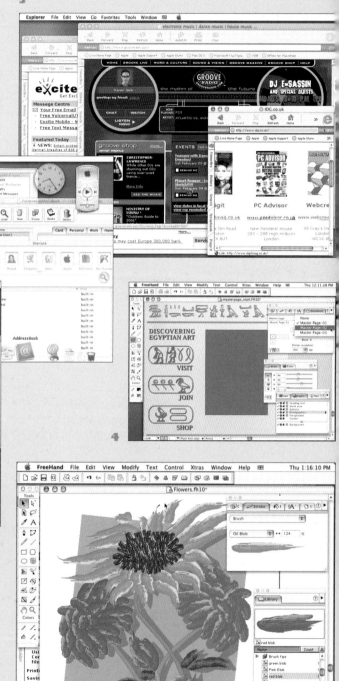

1 | 2 | 3 | 4 | 5

Apple's Mac OS X (1–5) was the first operating system to offer a vision of how glorious a boring old computer desktop could become. The Aqua interface of the first X releases includes an animated Dock along the bottom that reacts to mouse-over and click actions to provide tactile feedback. Drop-down menus have been given shaded effects, and there's an overall soft, transparent feel that, if anything, goes against the grain of the industrial metallic fashion of the time.

6 | 7 | 8 | 9 | 10
Microsoft's Windows XP takes not only the dull gray edge off its world-leading PC operating system, but the corners, too. A coordinated business blue pervades the default interface, which should make casual users happy without completely upsetting the serious guys. For the determined, though, Windows XP can display the classic square gray interface again if required.

E-MAIL NEWSLETTERS

When subscribing to an e-mail newsletter, you are often asked whether you'd like the mailing to be pure text or HTML-formatted. Sometimes it pays to pick the latter option, as these examples show. The only limitations are that you have to be on-line in order for the images to appear, and e-mail software is obviously slower than a Web browser at processing and displaying HTML.

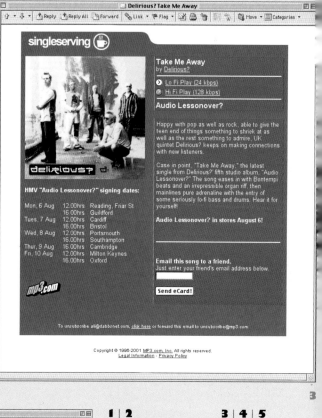

1 | 2

SurfEurope (1) and *Onboard* (2) magazines tell you when the latest print issue is out by using a clean layout and relatively small graphics that won't clog up your modem.

3 | 4 | 5

The biggest proponents of e-mail newsletters are Web-based operations, and some of the best belong to the music download sites. mp3.com (3) uses tabs, as if the band in question has been pulled out of a card index file. MusicMatch (4) has tried two different formats here: one stretching the tabbed card idea, and the other (5) following a more conventional, Web-like magazine layout.

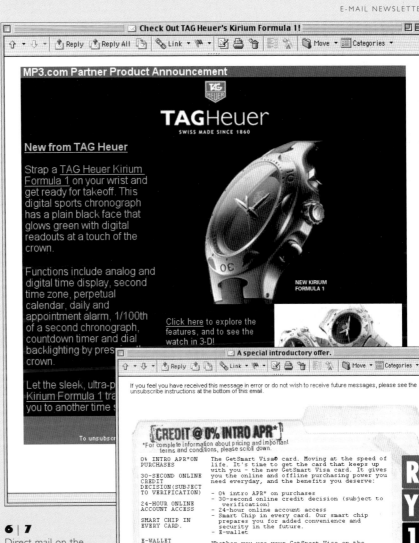

6 | 7

Direct mail on the Internet—"spam"—doesn't have to be unwelcome if it looks good. TAG Heuer (6) promotes its watches in a production style reminiscent of TV advertisements, and you can also link to 3D models of the watches. And GetSmart Visa (7) demonstrates how selling cheap credit needn't look cheap.

FOR MORE INFORMATION . . .

Presenting large amounts of complex information is a real challenge for the interface designer. The Sky Digital television service (near right and below) offers one solution: a button on the remote control handset calls up a well-constructed menu, with four initial video feeds from which to choose. Any of the feeds can be previewed, or they can be run singly in a larger window. One may also browse through the text-based news, keeping the broadcast feed in a small pane. The PDF (opposite) is another solution to this problem.

1

2

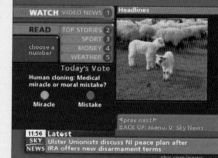

1 | 2 | 3 | 4

You can see in these screen images an interesting use of the Digibox's (1) landline phone link, which allows viewers to respond to quick polls interactively and see immediate results. What makes Sky News Active unique is the way it crams a large amount of information into an interface hierarchy that is never more than three levels (2, 3, 4) deep, and that remains intuitive to the beginner.

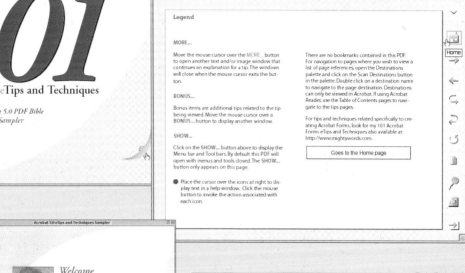

139

5 | 6 | 7

Adobe Acrobat PDF (5) is very much underrated as a distributable presentation format, but that's mostly because people churn out PDFs without understanding what they're for or what they're actually capable of. Technical author and PDF guru Ted Padova puts theory into practice by giving away a sampler of his Acrobat 5.0 tips ... in PDF format (6, 7). But instead of being the usual electronic paper document, this one incorporates its own navigation interface. It's hardly cutting-edge graphic design, but it provides a thoroughly practical approach for a highly misunderstood format.

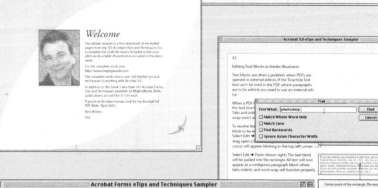

8 | 9 | 10

When the viewer's mouse pointer (8) hovers over any of the navigation buttons down the right, a tool tip appears and an explanation is given in a yellow panel on the first page (9). The document contains internal and external links, incorporates pop-up notes, and supports both Destinations and a search function (10).

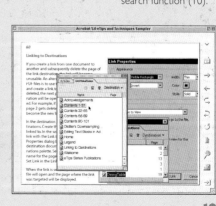

WEB MULTIMEDIA

Animation and video on the Internet rarely exist in isolation. People should be provided with controls for playing and managing movies. Look at how Web multimedia is framed with special interfaces—themselves animated in most cases—to make the experience richer and easier for casual Web visitors.

140

2

When you select one of the TV buttons, you expect to get an instant video stream, which is what BBC World provides. However, this is quite rare now.

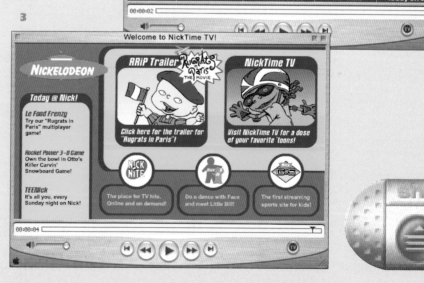

1

This is what you see if you click on the TV button of the QuickTime Player interface: a collection of media-content suppliers who have streaming QuickTime media feeds available.

3 | 4 | 5

What you usually get is a colorful and appealing little page (3) for that particular content provider. Some of this content will trigger video streams (4), but much of it links to conventional Web pages in your default Web browser (5). This effectively turns QuickTime Player into a miniature button palette for your Web site's latest content.

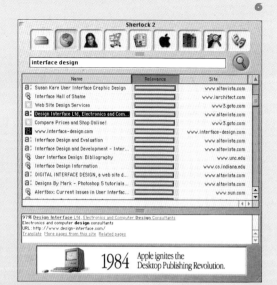

6

Apple's Sherlock 2 Web search tool has also been given the brushed aluminum look. As with QuickTime, it animates when you change the tab or program mode. Viewers are now beginning to expect animation effects when clicking on things, and not a straight flip from one thing to another.

141

7

Macromedia's ShockMachine is a utility for storing ShockWave games and presentations on your hard disk so that they can be located and played back later without you having to go back on-line. Note the aluminum look again, and the way the interface animates— the games are stored on a carousel that appears to rotate as you browse the titles.

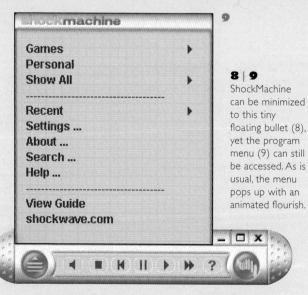

8 | 9

ShockMachine can be minimized to this tiny floating bullet (8), yet the program menu (9) can still be accessed. As is usual, the menu pops up with an animated flourish.

CREATIVE TOOLS

2

Back in the 1990s, a certain Kai Krause was upsetting the desktop computing apple cart worldwide by working on his own interface revolution. He saw boxy gray operating systems as a major limitation to creative expression and entertainment. He also saw rapidly increasing computing power and plummeting memory prices as keys to unlock the escape hatch. The result was a whole string of best-selling professional and consumer graphics software products, most of which ended up under the MetaCreations banner, which has since split up and been sold off.

142

1

1 | 2 | 3

Among the surviving products of Krause's fertile mind is the Photoshop plug-in suite Kai's Power Tools (KPT). The idea behind these image filters was to turn whatever it is you're trying to do into a voyage of discovery. Often the tools don't seem to make sense: you just click on things and drag them around while bizarre colors and shapes swirl around inside the preview window. Kai taught us that predictability is the killer of creativity. It's interesting to see that now, ten years later, the operating system giants are finally coming around to his point of view.

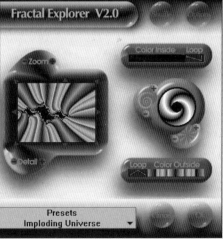

3

4 | 5

Corel bought up the rights to MetaCreations' Bryce and went on to issue an update that remains reasonably faithful to the original interface concept. Bryce is a 3D program for creating dramatic wide-angle scenes and landscapes, but it does not use anything that even remotely resembles a conventional 3D modeling or rendering interface. The main editing tool bar across the top offers three modes, whose functions are self-explanatory thanks to the graphic nature of the buttons.

6

Basic navigation around a scene is handled by dragging on the various directional arrows on the left. Animation tools are arranged across the bottom.

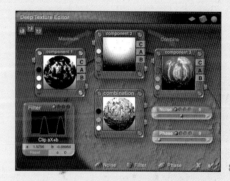

143

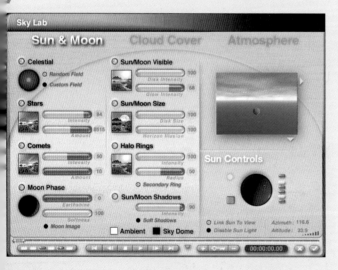

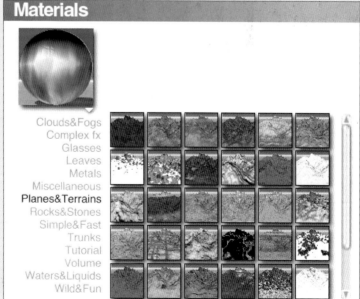

7 | 8 | 9

Sure, this program makes use of dialogue boxes like any other, but just look at them. Program tools and dialogues don't need to look like this, but the Bryce team has gone and done it anyway in order to make 3D design an entertaining, experimental, and pleasant experience for the non-technical artist. If only they could do the same for word processors.

SAVING SPACE

Adobe, the manufacturer of the tremendously successful Photoshop application, holds a number of patents on tabbed palette interfaces, and their flexibility has won a lot of praise over the years. Here is an example of how their innovative design works in favor of the computer user.

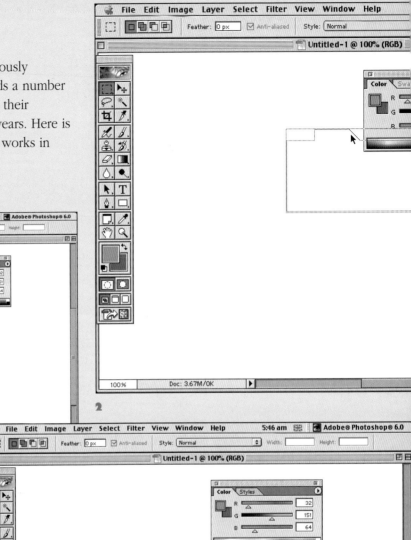

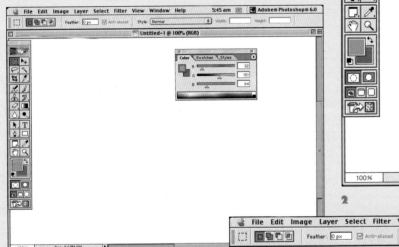

1

This is how the screen looks when the Color palette is first called up in Photoshop.

2

Suppose you want to work with the Color and Swatches palettes at the same time, which indeed many people do. Click on the Swatches tab and drag it to one side.

3

The Swatches tab has been torn away and now floats as an independent palette with its own title bar.

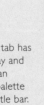

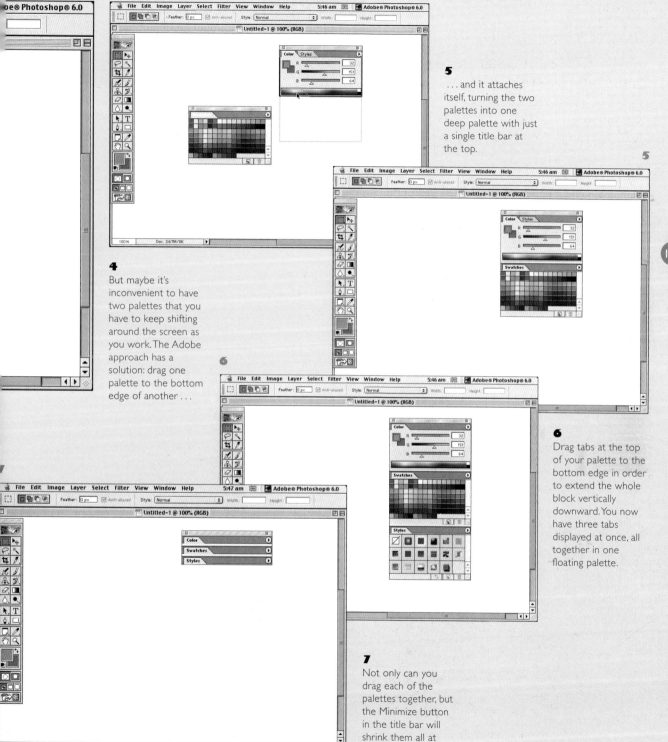

4

5
. . . and it attaches itself, turning the two palettes into one deep palette with just a single title bar at the top.

5

145

4
But maybe it's inconvenient to have two palettes that you have to keep shifting around the screen as you work. The Adobe approach has a solution: drag one palette to the bottom edge of another . . .

6

6
Drag tabs at the top of your palette to the bottom edge in order to extend the whole block vertically downward. You now have three tabs displayed at once, all together in one floating palette.

7

7
Not only can you drag each of the palettes together, but the Minimize button in the title bar will shrink them all at once, too.

WINAMP

Software that supports the concept of "skins" leaves the door open to creative designers to customize how that software looks and operates. The ability to run third-party (and generally free) skins is what made WinAmp the most successful MP3 and CD audio player program on the Windows platform in the early days of MP3 development. Enjoy this tiny sampling of the thousands (literally) of WinAmp skins available across the Internet, which have been created by amateur enthusiasts and professional designers alike.

1 — 15

1 Hi-tech trash
2 Sun skin
3 Pochacco blue
4 Summer breeze
5 Jade in jade
6 Paper amp
7 Harvest moon
8 Mdk-2
9 Croq-amp
10 Connect-x
11 Blue silver
12 Blood and gold
13 Fish thauses
14 Hand-written
15 Boxster amp

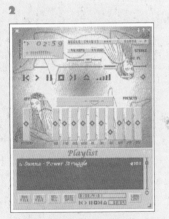

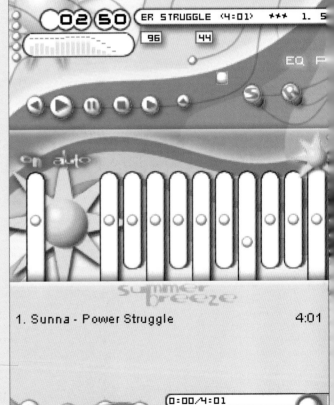

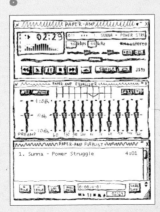

7

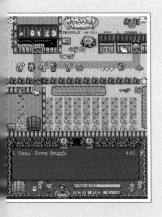

8

9

10

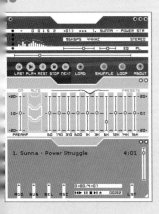

11

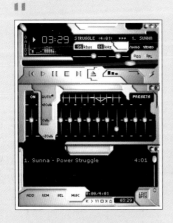

12

13

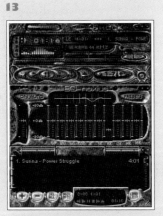

14

15

MUSICMATCH JUKEBOX

Since the success of WinAmp and its skins, a whole genre of customizable audio and video player utilities has appeared on the commercial and freeware market, for PC and Mac alike. People also wanted players that could be minimized to just the core playback buttons or expanded to allow access to the full feature set. This gave rise to dual-design skins, an example of which is the commercial product MusicMatch Jukebox.

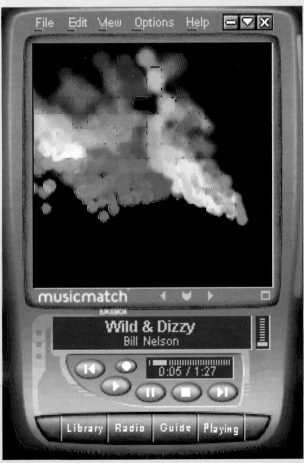

148

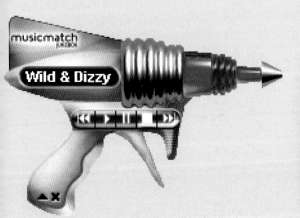

WINDOWS MEDIA PLAYER

Microsoft bundles its own audio and video player utility with its Windows operating system. Windows Media Player comes with a variety of skins as standard, but you can download many more. Most of them appear to be created by Microsoft, but there are plenty from design agencies and individuals, too, that include winners of international skin design competitions. (Windows Media Player applies skin overlays only when it is in minimized mode.)

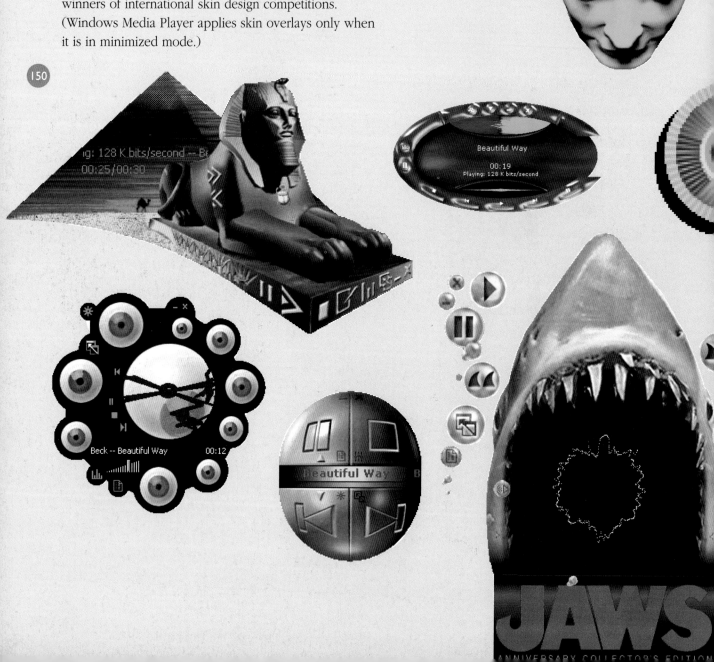

151

< bits/second -- Media

00:48
01:31:00

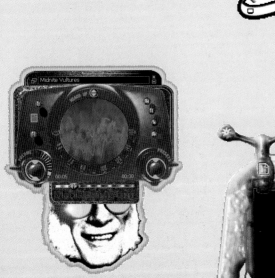

Midnite Vultures

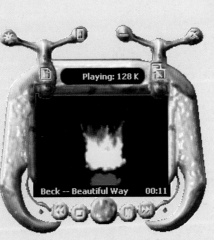

Playing: 128 K

Beck -- Beautiful Way   00:11

Y'S TAVERN   Media   00:30

SONIQUE

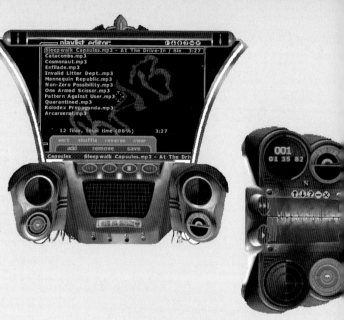

Let's round up our showcase of skins with an audio player utility called Sonique. Although it's free, Sonique is the most powerful program of its kind when it comes to support for skins. It may not operate any faster or sound any better than other MP3 and CD players, but the sheer variety and creative imagination that this one program has encouraged in skin designers is awesome. It's also unusual because it has three visual size modes rather than just two, although we've only shown the medium and full sizes here—the tiny size tends to be visually plain and minimalist because it's supposed to be.

152

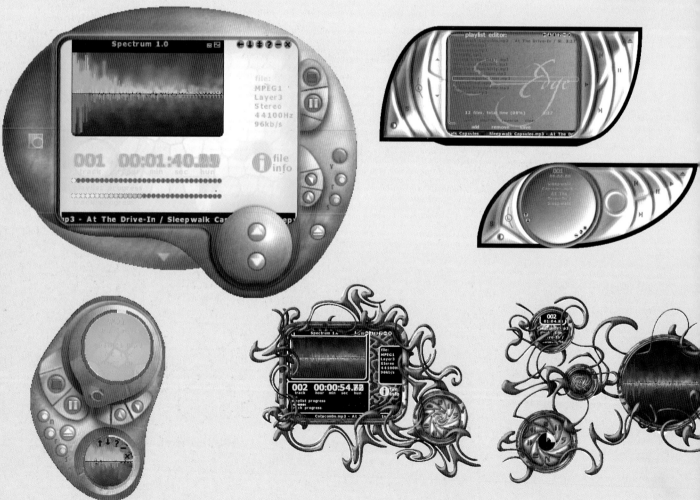

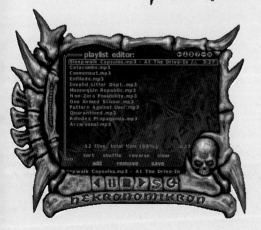

SONIQUE II

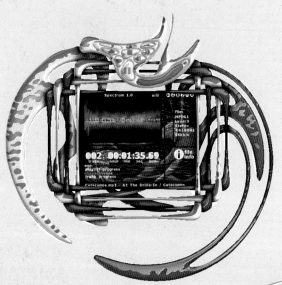

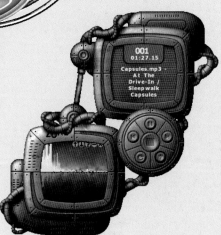

FLASH IDEAS

As part of the "Montréal en Lumière" city festival, the organizers wanted to put a site map on its Web site (www.montrealenlumiere.com). They could have used a standard street map, but the intention wasn't to show street names so much as to indicate what events were taking place and where. The images on this page show how they went about it. Opposite, Tecsys opted not to promote its FullStream e-commerce solution using the bland tricks available to HTML programmers. Instead, they have chosen to use a distributable presentation that has been painstakingly created in Flash. The images on the facing page illustrate this project.

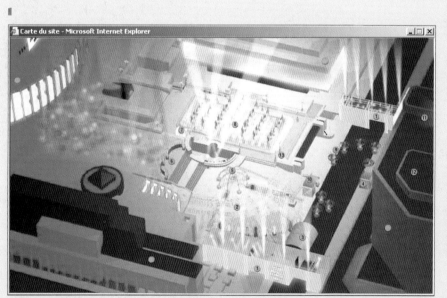

1 | 2 | 3 | 4 | 5

This slick and deceptively simple Flash presentation was commissioned to fit the brief. Initially (1), it shows a three-quarter isometric diagram of the city, dotted with numbered circles that mark the venues. If you pass your mouse over any circle, the city darkens, while the venue you have just picked stays highlighted and event details are listed (2–5). If you have trouble viewing the image, you can zoom in and out using right-click menus and also drag to pan around.

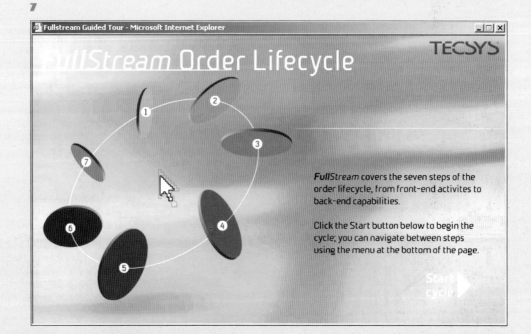

6 | 7 | 8 | 9 | 10

For those accessing the FullStream presentation over the Web, there's plenty of warning about the need for Flash, the file sizes, and the inevitable "Skip intro" button (6). The show kicks off with an opening screen that helpfully provides links to each of the seven steps, if you want to jump ahead (7). Each step includes lively animation without any hanging around (8–9). Skipping to later steps is quick, too. The last screen in the show (10) makes it very clear that it's the last, and also provides "back to start" and Web site links. There's not too much text here either, which helps to focus the viewer's attention on the four button choices at the bottom.

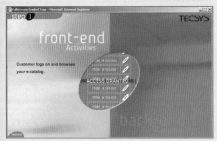

CANADARM2 ON-LINE

The Canadarm2 project was a major technical success for the Canadian Space Agency in 2001, as well as being a huge media hit in the country. Members of the public were encouraged to learn more about the agency's involvement in the development of the international space station by exploring certain topics on its Web site, which were presented with 3D interfaces.

1 | 2 | 3
Call up the spaceman and rotate him in . . . well . . . space.

4 | 5 | 6
Click on his helmet to zoom into a close-up model, open the visor, and find out more information.

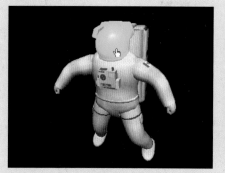

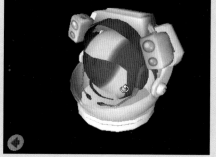

4

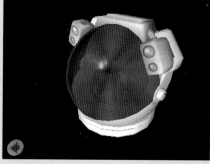

5

6

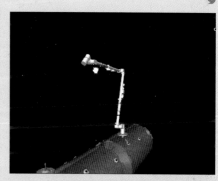

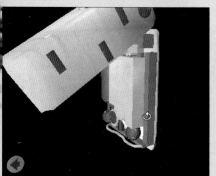

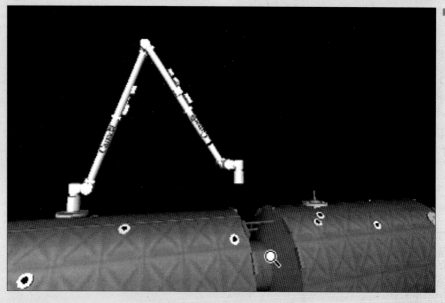

7 | 8
Click on his backpack
to see it in more
detail, open it up, and
have a look inside.

9 | 10
The Canadarm2 is a
3D model that is
manipulated using
"hot points." The arm
moves with a realistic
kinetic motion, and
you can rotate the
screen if it helps you
to see what's
happening. The idea
is to lock the arm
down with a grapple
fixture, like a simple
computer game.

BBC VIRTUAL WORLDS

The BBC's history department has turned a number of its key reconstructions into VRML scenes that can be accessed on the Web. All that's required is Parallel Graphics' free Cortona plug-in to view them.

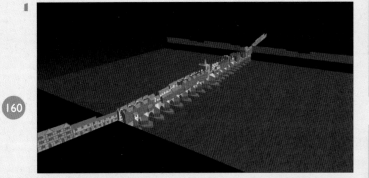

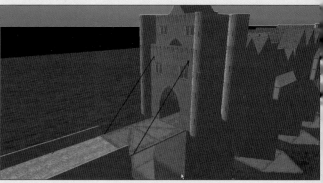

1 | 2 | 3 | 4 | 5
It's not a complete virtual world, but the BBC has made a very practical job of this reconstruction of the old London Bridge. Normally, even Londoners get to see the bridge like this only in contemporary etchings and museum models, but now anyone can go for a walk across it in cyberspace.

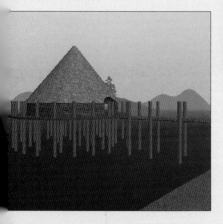

10

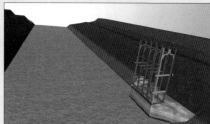

11

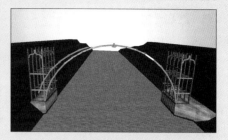

12

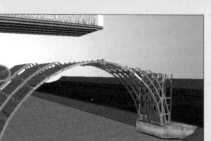

10 | 11 | 12 | 13 | 14

In this project, the BBC wanted to demonstrate how Telford's original Ironbridge was constructed. The initial building sequence is a self-running animation, after which you can explore the architecture from underneath or stroll across the top.

13

14

6 | 7 | 8 | 9

Here the viewer gets to experience what it might have been like to paddle up to a Crannog-style river house on stilts in ancient Scotland. The viewer can roam the banks, join the animated boatman as he takes a tour around the little islands, or enter the hut to see what's inside.

Click on the door to load the next world

WELLCOME WING

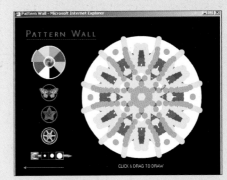

The Wellcome Wing at London's Science Museum is a themed interactive exhibition over four floors, providing multimedia presentations and lively showcases at every module. The Museum's Web site hosts a near-perfect VRML copy of the Wellcome Wing and its exhibits. Each floor covers a different theme—in the full 3D scenes you can walk around the floors and in between modules as well as look around at the current exhibitions. Clicking on the main items produces pop-up windows that variously contain QuickTime VR graphics, interactive Flash movies, and HTML introductions.

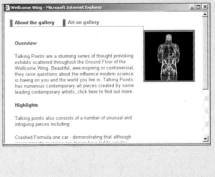

INTERACTIVE 3D

MAN Roland, a printing manufacturer, distributes training and maintenance manuals to its customers. Here, though, the company has used VRML technology from Parallel Graphics to produce an interactive 3D version of one of its manuals (this page). Meanwhile, Fira Cosmetics (facing page) has noticed that you can update colors and components in Cult3D, and this has resulted in some tactile presentations for its e-commerce set-up.

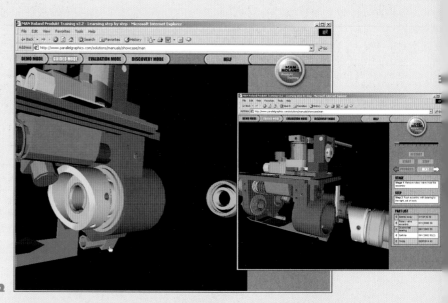

2

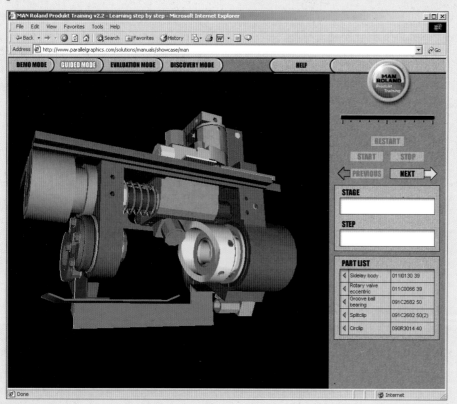

1

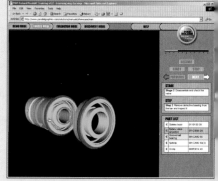

4

1 | 2 | 3 | 4

This series explains how to replace the rotary valve from an engine assembly. You are prompted each step of the way with text instructions while the next component that you need to remove flashes on-screen. You click on this to watch it move away, and then the scene swivels around to offer a better view for the next step. Alternatively, you can interact directly with the model in 3D space. No printed manual could possibly compare with this.

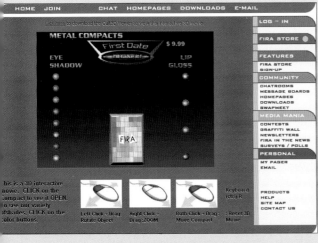

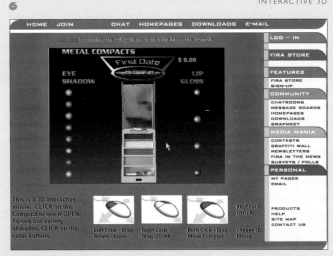

5 | 6 | 7 | 8
Note how once you open up this metallic compact case, the mirror inside the cover appears to reflect "your" face back to you. It's just a simple reflection map, but isn't it a great idea, and flattering to the prospective buyer, too? Clicking on the colored circles on either side changes the content of the makeup.

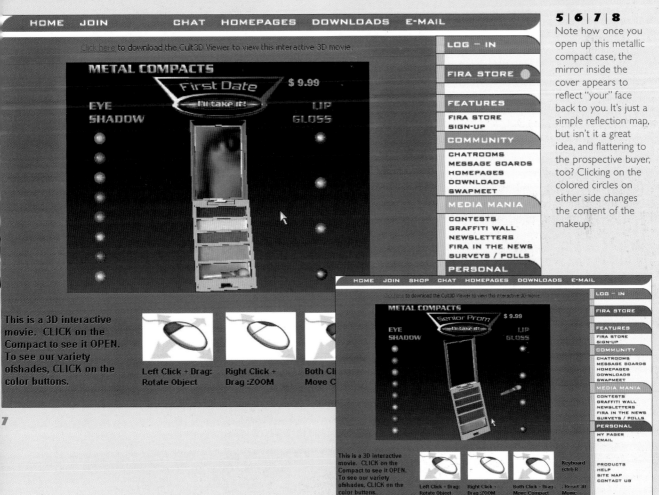

E-COMMERCE

It has become a cliché, but it is nevertheless true that e-commerce is one of the Internet's "killer applications." A photo-realistic model of a product doesn't necessarily command more interest than the hundreds of other 3D-enabled shopping malls on the Internet, but here are some examples of innovative designs that have grabbed users' imaginations.

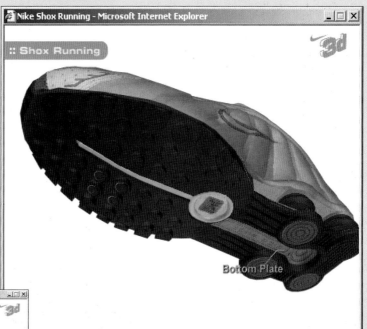

1 | 2
Nike's inclusion of annotations in the Viewpoint format, which appear and vanish as you rotate the shoe in space, is a useful addition.

3 | 4 | 5
The designer has also made good use of the space by including a row of menu-like tabs at the bottom of the small window. The tabs reveal big, clear buttons and thumbnails that most viewers will find perfectly intuitive. Few will be able to look through the tabs without clicking on the irresistible "Animations" button.

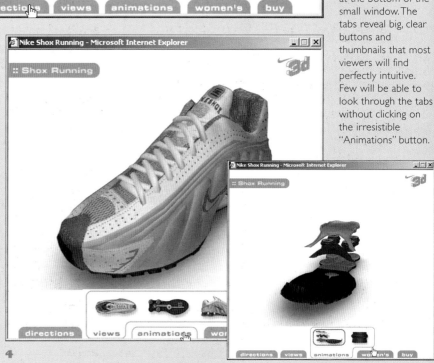

6 | 7 | 8 | 9 | 10

Virtual Air Sites employs iPIX technology to present a neat mix of still photographs and panoramas within the Aerial View section of its Web site. The viewer clicks on a summit or other highlighted point in the still image, and this opens an iPIX panorama in a pane to the right. This way, viewers always know where they are.

ROALDDAHL.COM

The increasing worldwide popularity of author Roald
Dahl has led to the creation of this dedicated Web
site, which is primarily aimed at children. It's entirely
Flash-based and includes little animated sequences to
keep viewers busy while they are waiting for the next
section to download.

1 | 2
An interesting
approach is taken
with the graphics,
which barely stop
moving. This produces
an amusingly chaotic
feel without having
too many graphics

on-screen at one
time. Bugs, birds, and
animals constantly
make their way across
the screen in DHTML
layers, deliberately
getting in the way.

3 | 4
Pass the mouse over
a TV set and a face
appears. Click on it
and a unique item of
Roald Dahl-related
news appears in a
scrollable pane.

5 | 6
You can pick a book character to act as your guide through the site. The character then appears at the top right of certain pages, and his or her voice tells you what to do. (You need to keep your speakers turned on, of course, in order for this to work.)

7 | 8 | 9 | 10 | 11 | 12
Ah, you've found the games. I knew you would.

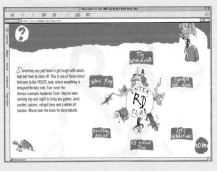

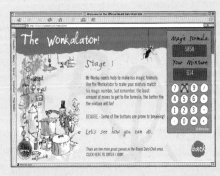

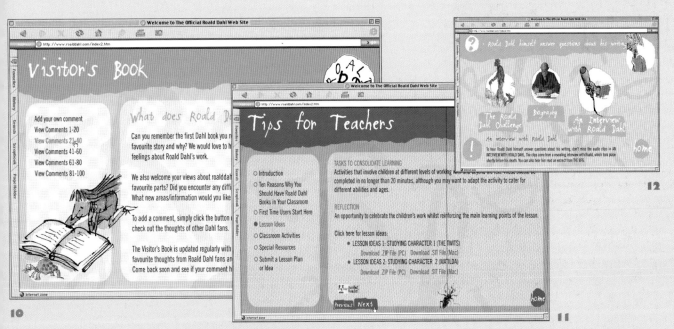

LONG AND WIDE WEB

As previous sections of this book have made clear, in general it's a good idea to avoid forcing the viewer to scroll too far downward or too far across in order to see content. However, rules are made to be broken, and in certain contexts, very wide or very deep pages can perform useful functions.

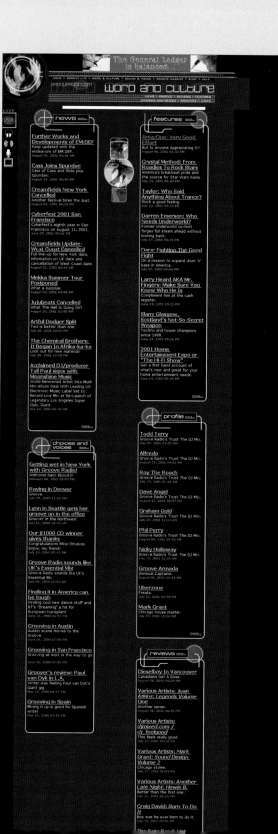

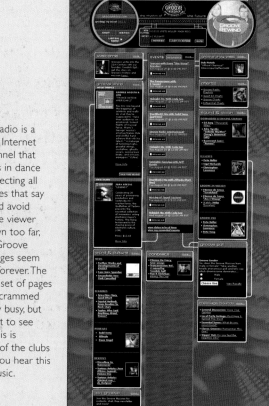

1 | 2

Groove Radio is a California Internet radio channel that specializes in dance music. Rejecting all design rules that say you should avoid making the viewer scroll down too far, some of Groove Radio's pages seem to go on forever. The result is a set of pages that feels crammed and overly busy, but offers a lot to see and do. This is evocative of the clubs in which you hear this kind of music.

3 **4** **5** **6** **7**

Leading print manufacturer Heidelberg's Web site wants you to think horizontally rather than vertically. Jump lists and pop-up menus are rejected in favor of a progressive hierarchy diagram that stretches out toward the right. The arrow pointing back on the last screen shown here links back to the previous page.

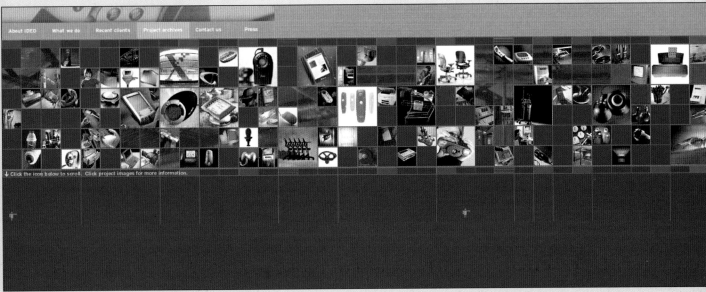

8

Industrial design studio Ideo presents its portfolio as a wide, horizontally scrolling page of thumbnails. The little "man pointing" figures are actually buttons that scroll the page across in your Web browser.

NAVIGATION IDEAS

The real Guinness Storehouse in Dublin is quite a big museum. The Flash movie for the store at the Guinness Web site is not a virtual tour by any means, but it's quite amusing. The images on the facing page demonstrate that it's possible for designers to produce content-heavy sites that can be viewed on a small screen.

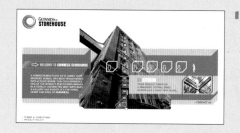

1

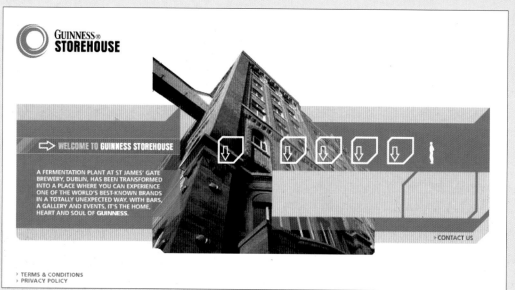

2

1 | 2 | 3 | 4 | 5 | 6 | 7 | 8
The movie fits neatly into a very small window, the site uses floating objects as buttons, and the pint-glass loading graphic is a nice touch.

172

3

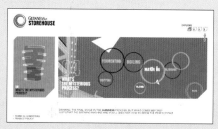

4

5

6

7

8

9 | 10 | 11 | 12 | 13
These sites think small on the outside (page size), but big on the inside (content). By cramming as much as possible into that sub-640 x 480 pixel area, successful sites can guarantee that users will see their entire home page without scrolling.

173

12

13

FRESH FACES

Refusing to conform to some of the rules of conventional interface design isn't necessarily a bad thing. So long as there's a reason for doing what you do, it's possible to spurn buttons and scrollbars and replace them with a completely fresh interface. See how these Web sites have freed themselves from graphical baggage.

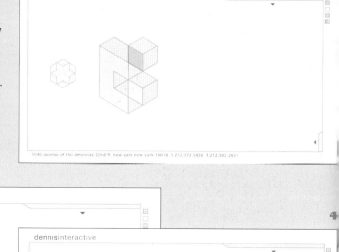

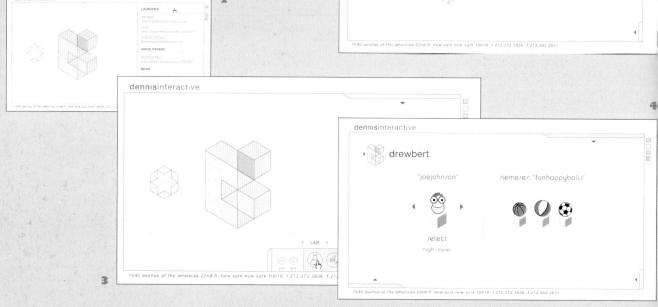

1 | 2 | 3 | 4
Sometimes designers will do anything to ease the constraints that a Web browser imposes. One company to do this is Dennis Interactive, whose Web pages are visually minimalist, self-contained Flash movies. Passing a mouse over the little arrows causes menu items and tools to expand into the interface, after which they zip straight back up into nowhere.

5 | 6
There are no prizes, then, for guessing that BThere's site was put together by Dennis Interactive. Once again, it relieves the user of menus and browser buttons. Instead, the interface provides huge, chunky buttons and animated expanding menus, which are enough to make you forget your old dull gray Web browser. Special items are launched in pop-up windows.

174

7 | 8 | 9

G-Shock knows that if you set your mind on something, you'll find a way to make it happen. Here, it was a matter of designing a set of promotional Web pages that look as though they're shaped like one of G-Shock's own watches. But the company didn't want to put viewers off with lots of Flash code, so they offer HTML and Flash versions of the same site, with as much similarity between them as possible.

175

8

10

Just to prove the point, here's a page from the HTML edition. Spot the differences.

10

9

MTV2

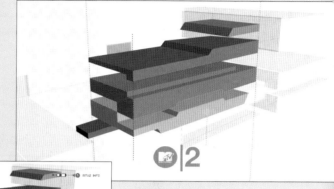

The legendary—Flash-based—MTV2 Web site employs the same graphics as the music channel. After a while, you realize that none of the buttons look like buttons. It's part of the industrial/outsider appeal of the channel. Objects bounce when the mouse pointer passes over them. Each color-coded section of the site is introduced with a few seconds of animation, although this is not repeated on subsequent returns to those pages (which would have been a classic annoying interface blunder). Nothing is more than two levels deep, so there's no real need for a "Back" button: just click on the colored cubes at the bottom of each screen to jump to any section of the main screen.

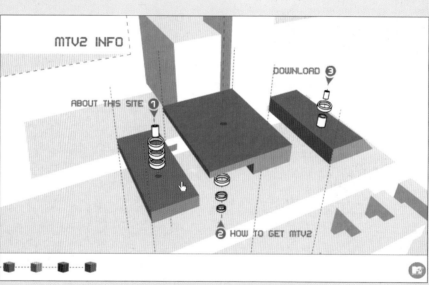

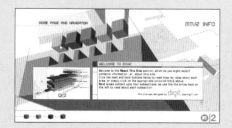

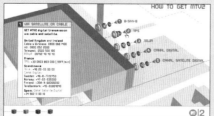

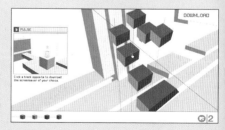

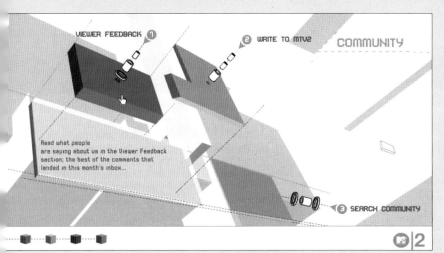

VIEWER FEEDBACK ①   ② WRITE TO MTV2   COMMUNITY

Read what people
are saying about us in the Viewer Feedback
section; the best of the comments that
landed in this month's inbox...

③ SEARCH COMMUNITY

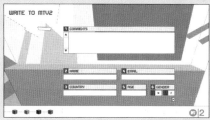

WRITE TO MTV2

VIEWER
FEEDBACK   WRITE TO MTV2

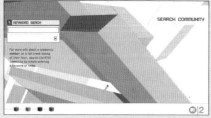

SEARCH COMMUNITY

KEYWORD SEARCH

177

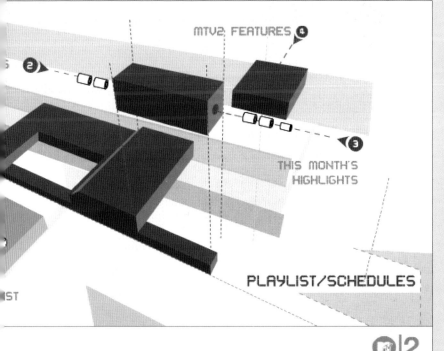

②   MTV2 FEATURES ④

③

THIS MONTH'S
HIGHLIGHTS

PLAYLIST/SCHEDULES

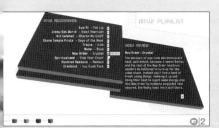

MTV2 PLAYLIST

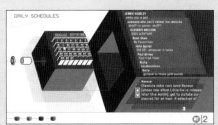

DAILY SCHEDULES

THIS MONTH'S
HIGHLIGHTS

GLOSSARY · 180

INDEX · 189

178

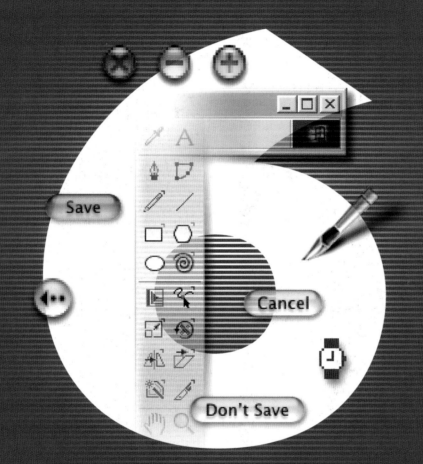

GLOSSARY

3D *abbr.:* three dimensional—that is, an effect that gives the illusion of depth on a flat page or monitor.

absolute URL A complete address, or "uniform resource locator (URL), which takes you to a specific location in a Web site rather than to the home page of the site. An absolute URL will contain the full file path to the page document location on the host server, for example: http://yoursite.com/extrainfo/aboutyou/yourhouse.htm

active hyperlink A currently selected word or button that forms a link to another location, often differentiated from other links on the same page by a different color.

ActiveX Microsoft's proprietary technology for creating interactive Web pages. ActiveX controls are not platform-independent and are mainly supported only in Microsoft Windows environments.

Adobe Acrobat A proprietary "portable document format" (PDF) file, which has fonts and pictures embedded in the document, enabling it to be viewed and printed on different computer systems.

aliasing The term used to describe the jagged appearance commonly seen in bitmapped images or fonts, either when the resolution is insufficient or when they have been enlarged. This is caused by the pixels—which are square with straight sides—making up the image becoming visible.

alignment The placement of type or images so that they line up according to an invisible line, either horizontally or vertically.

anchor A text or graphic element that has an HTML tag that either links it to another location or that acts as a destination for an incoming link.

animated GIF A "GIF" (graphics interchange format) file comprised of multiple images, simulating an animation when played back in a Web browser.

animation A process of creating a moving image by rapidly moving from one still image to the next. Traditionally, this was achieved through a laborious process of drawing or painting each "frame" manually onto cellulose acetate sheets ("cels," or "cells"). However, animations are now more usually created with specialzed software that renders sequences in a variety of formats, typically QuickTime, AVI, and animated GIFs.

antialias/antialiasing A technique of optically eliminating the jagged effect of bitmapped images or text reproduced on low-resolution devices such as monitors. This is achieved by adding pixels of an in-between tone—the edges of the object's color are blended with its background by averaging the density of the range of pixels involved. Antialiasing is also sometimes employed to filter texture maps, such as those used in 3D applications, to prevent moiré patterns.

applet Although a general term that can be applied to any small application that performs a specific task, such as the calculator, an applet is usually used to describe a small application written in the Java programming language, which is downloaded by an Internet browser to perform specific tasks.

ascender The part of a lowercase character which extends above its body ("x-height"), as in the letters b, d, f, g, h, k, l, t.

ASCII (*pron.:* asskee) *acronym:* American Standard Code for Information Interchange, a code used to assign individual numbers to 256 letters, numbers, and symbols (including carriage returns and tabs) that can be typed on a keyboard. ASCII is the cross-platform, computer industry-standard, text-only file format.

aspect ratio The ratio of the width of an image to its height, expressed as x:y. For example, the aspect ratio of an image measuring 200 × 100 pixels is 2:1.

attachment An external file, such as an image or text document, "attached" to an email message for electronic transmission.

attribute (1) A characteristic of an HTML tag that is identified alongside the tag in order to describe it.

attribute (2) The specification applied to a character, box, or other item. Character attributes include font, size, style, color, shade, scaling, kerning, etc.

authoring tool/application/software/program Software that enables the user to create interactive presentations such as those used in multimedia titles and Web sites. Authoring programs typically provide text, drawing, painting, animation, and audio features, and combine these with a scripting language that determines how each element of the page or screen behaves, such as an instruction contained within a button to tell the computer to display a different page or perform a specific task—like play a movie, for example.

background The area of an image upon which the principal subject, or foreground, sits.

bandwidth The measure of the speed at which information is passed between two points, which may be between modems, or across a "bus," or from memory to disk—the broader the bandwidth, the faster data flows.

banner An image on a Web page, usually at the top, that deliberately attracts attention, generally for advertising purposes.

base alignment The alignment of type characters of differing sizes or fonts along their baselines.

baseline The imaginary line, defined by the flat base of a lowercase letter such as "x," upon which the bases of all upper and lowercase letters apparently rest.

binary code The computer code, using 1 or 0, that is used to represent a character or instruction. For example, the binary code 01100010 represents a lowercase "b."

binary file A file that is described in binary code rather than text. Binary files typically hold pictures, sounds, or a complete application program.

binary system Numbering system that uses two digits, 0 and 1, as distinct from the decimal system of 0–9.

bit Acronym for binary digit, the smallest piece of information a computer can use. A bit is expressed as one of two values, which can be a 1 or a 0, on or off, something or nothing, negative or positive, small or large, etc. Each alphabetical character requires eight bits (called a "byte") to store it.

bit depth Describes the number of bits assigned to each pixel on a monitor, scanner, or image file. One-bit, for example, will only produce black and white (the bit is either on or off), whereas 8-bit will generate 256 grays or colors (256 is the maximum number of permutations of a string of eight 1s and 0s), and 24-bit will produce 16.7 million colors (256 × 256 × 256).

bit map/bitmap Strictly speaking, any text character or image comprised of dots. A bit map is a "map" of "bits" that describes the complete collection of the bits that represent the location and binary state (on or off) of a corresponding set of items, such as pixels, which are required to form an image, such as on a display monitor.

bitmapped graphic An image made up of dots or pixels, and usually generated by "paint" or "image-editing" applications, as distinct from the "vector" images of "object-oriented" drawing applications.

bit rate The speed at which data is transmitted across communications channels, measured in bits per second (bps). Sometimes erroneously referred to as baud rate.

body One of the structures of HTML documents, falling between headers and footers.

browser An application enabling you to view or "browse" World Wide Web pages across the Internet.

button An interface control, usually appearing in dialogue boxes, that you click to designate, confirm, or cancel an action. Default buttons are those that are usually emphasized by a heavy border and that can be activated by the "enter" or "return" keys.

byte A single group that is made up of eight bits (0s and 1s) and is processed by a computer as one unit. It is possible to configure eight 0s and 1s in only 256 different permutations, thus a byte can represent any value between 0 and 255—the maximum number of ASCII characters, for example, one byte being required for each.

C++ A mainstream programming language.

CAD (acronym: computer-aided design) Any design carried out using a computer.

However, the term is generally used with reference to 3D design, such as product design or architecture, where a computer software application is used to construct and develop complex structures.

cap height The height of a capital letter, measured from its baseline.

cell A space containing information in the rows or columns of a table.

character On a computer, any single letter, number, punctuation mark, or symbol represented by 8 bits (1 byte), including invisible characters such as "space," "return," and "tab."

child (object) An object linked hierarchically to another object (its "parent"). For example, when a "child" box is placed within—or linked to—a "parent" box, then when the latter is moved, the child—and all its "grandchildren!"—move with it, retaining their relative positions and orientation. This enables manipulation of complex structures, particularly in 3D applications.

clip art/clip media Collections of (usually) royalty-free photographs, illustrations, graphics, design devices, and other pre-created items such as movies, sounds, and 3D wireframes. Clip art is available in three forms—on paper that can be cut out and pasted onto camera-ready art, on computer disk, or, increasingly, via the Web.

color depth The number of bits required to define the color of each pixel. For example, only one bit is required to display a black-and-white image (it is either on or off), whereas an 8-bit image can display either 256 grays or 256 colors, and a 24-bit image displays 16.7 million colors—eight bits each for red, green, and blue (256 × 256 × 256).

color gamut Gamut, or color space, describes the full range of colors achievable by any single device on the reproduction chain. While the visible spectrum contains many millions of colors, not all of them are achievable by all devices, and, even if the color gamuts for different devices overlap, they will never match exactly—for example, the 16.7 million colors that can be displayed on a monitor cannot be printed on a commercial four-color press. For this reason, various color

management systems (CMS) have been devised to maintain consistency of color gamuts across various devices.

color library An application support file containing predefined colors. These may be the default colors, colors defined by you, or other predefined color palettes or tables.

color management module A profile for managing and matching colors accurately across different platforms and devices. CMMs conform to a color management system (CMS) such as that defined by the International Color Consortium (ICC). CMMs interpret the ICC profiles, which describe the RGB and CMYK color spaces on your computer. There are usually existing ICC profiles that are installed on your computer by ICC-compliant applications such as Adobe Photoshop, or you can create your own. The selected profile is then embedded in the image you are working on so that it can later be used as a reference by other devices in the production process.

color management system The name given to a method devised to provide accuracy and consistency of color representation across all devices in the color reproduction chain—scanners, monitors, printers, etc. Typical CMSs are those defined by the International Color Consortium (ICC), Kodak's Digital Science Color Management System, Apple's ColorSync, and Microsoft's ICM.

color picker The term used to describe a color model that is displayed on a computer monitor. Color pickers may be specific to an application such as Adobe Photoshop, a third-party color model such as PANTONE, or to the operating system running on your computer.

ColorSync Apple Computer's implementation of the ICC standard.

color table A predefined table, or "index," of colors used to determine a specific color model, for example, for converting an image to CMYK. A color table, or "CLUT," also describes the palette of colors used to display an image.

complementary colors On a color wheel, two colors directly opposite each other that, when combined, form white or black depending on the color model (subtractive or additive).

compression The technique of rearranging data so that it either occupies less space on disk or transfers faster between devices or on communication lines. Different kinds of compression techniques are employed for different kinds of data—applications, for example, must not lose any data when compressed, whereas photographic images and movies can tolerate a certain amount of data loss. Compression methods that do not lose data are referred to as "lossless," whereas "lossy" is used to describe methods in which some data is lost. Movies and animations employ techniques called "codecs" (compression/decompression). There are many proprietary utilities for compressing data. Typical compression formats for images are LZW (lossless), JPEG and GIF (both lossy), the latter two being used commonly for files transmitted across the Internet.

computer graphics Strictly speaking, any graphic item generated on, or output by, a computer, such as page layouts, typography, illustrations, etc. However, the term is sometimes more specifically used to refer to a particular genre of computer-generated imagery, such as that which looks as though it were generated by computer.

console A videogame computer, typically hooked up to a domestic TV set. At the turn of the millennium, the most popular home computer in the world wasn't a PC or a Mac but a PlayStation.

content A generic term for any material that is being presented within an interface.

control panel A small application which enables you to configure system software or to customize various aspects of your computer, such as date, speaker volume, etc.

cross-platform The term that is applied to software, multimedia titles, or anything else (such as floppy disks) that have the capacity to work on more than one computer platform—that is, those that run different operating systems, such as the Macintosh OS or Microsoft Windows.

CSS *acronym:* cascading style sheets, the name for a specification sponsored by the World Wide Web Consortium for overcoming the limitations imposed by "classic HTML." Web designers (authors) have increasingly sought tools that would enable them to control every element of page design more tightly, with the result that the Web authoring community has developed unwieldy workarounds (such as using single-pixel GIF images to add character spacing), generating bulky HTML code that, in turn, resulted in longer downloads and browser incompatibilities. CSS allows the designer to exercise greater control over typography and layout in much the same way as he or she would expect in, say, a page-layout application, and provides the means of applying attributes such as font formats to paragraphs, parts of pages, or entire pages. Several style sheets can be applied to a single page, thus "cascading."

cursor The name for the blinking marker that indicates the current working position in a document—for example, the point in a line of text at which the next character will appear when you strike a key on the keyboard. The cursor may be represented by a small vertical line and is not to be confused with the "pointer"—the marker that indicates the current position of the mouse.

data Although strictly speaking the plural of "datum," meaning a piece of information, "data" is usually used as a singular noun to describe—particularly in the context of computers—more or less anything that can be stored or processed, whether it be a single bit, a chunk of text, an image, an audio file, and so on.

database Information that is stored on a computer in a systematic fashion and thus is retrievable. This generally means files where you store any amount of data in separate but consistent categories (called "fields") for each type of information such as names, addresses, and telephone numbers. The electronic version of a card index system (each card is called a "record"), databases are constructed with applications called "database managers," which allow you to organize information any way you like.

default The settings of a hardware device or software program that are determined at the time of manufacture or release. These settings remain in effect until you change them and your changes are stored—when applied to software—in a "preferences" file. Also called "presets" and "factory settings."

descender The part of a lowercase character that extends below the baseline of the x-height, as in the letters p, q, j, g, y.

desktop The generic term in a GUI for the background screen area upon which everything else sits, designating the visible working area of the interface. It can also be used to store files, folders, aliases, and shortcuts, and usually shows icons for storage devices.

desktop (publishing) system A collection of standard desktop hardware devices and off-the-shelf software applications capable of handling the entire desktop publishing process. As distinct from specialized equipment, such as drum scanners, used in high-end prepress systems.

DHTML see *DYNAMIC HTML*

dialogue box A box that appears on-screen requesting information or a decision before you can proceed further, such as the box that appears when you save a file, asking you what to call it and where to save it to.

dial-up The term describing a connection to the Internet or to a network that is made by dialing a telephone number for access.

digital Anything operated by or created from information represented by binary digits—such as in a digital recording—as distinct from analog, in which information is represented by a physical variable (in a recording this may be via the grooves in a vinyl platter).

digital data Information stored or transmitted as a series of 1s and 0s ("bits"). Because values are fixed (so-called "discrete values"), digital data is more reliable than analog, as the latter is susceptible to sometimes uncontrollable physical variations.

digitize, digitalize To convert anything, such as text, images, or sound, into binary form so that it can be digitally processed, manipulated, stored, and reconstructed.

dither(ing) The term describing a technique of "interpolation" which calculates the average value of adjacent pixels. This technique is used either to add extra pixels to an image—to smooth an edge, for example, as in "antialiasing"—or to reduce the number of colors or grays in an image by replacing them with average values that conform to a predetermined palette of colors, such as when an image containing millions of colors is converted ("resampled") to a fixed palette ("index") of, say, 256 colors—in Web use, for example. A color monitor operating in 8-bit color mode (256 colors) will automatically create a dithered pattern of pixels. Dithering is also used by some printing devices to simulate colors or tones.

document An all-encompassing description given to a file that contains information used by a computer user in the course of everyday work or play. Permission permitting, it can be opened, edited, and resaved. Word processor files, spreadsheets, pictures, movies, preferences files, settings files, and so on are documents. Programs, control panels, plug-in extensions, and so on are not.

DOS *acronym*: disk operating system. This term is now generically applied, for example, to MS-(Microsoft) DOS, Dr-DOS and many other rebranded systems that have appeared over the years. The original version was named QDOS—quick and dirty operating system.

download To transfer data from a remote computer—such as an Internet server—to your own. The opposite of *upload*.

dpi *acronym*: dots per inch.

draw(ing) application Drawing applications can be defined as those that are object-oriented (they use "vectors" to mathematically define lines and shapes), as distinct from painting applications, which use pixels to make images ("bitmapped graphics")—some applications do combine both.

drilling down The act of navigating deeper and deeper into a hierarchical structure, such as nested folders or multiple sub-menus.

driver/device driver A small piece of software that tells a computer how to handle or operate a piece of hardware, such as a printer, scanner, or disk drive. Depending on its function, a driver may be located within the operating system software and therefore loaded at start-up, or it may form a "plug-in" to an application (as do some scanner drivers, for example).

drop-down menu The menu that appears when you click on a title in the menu bar along the top of your screen. Also called "pop-down menu" or "pull-down menu."

Dynamic HTML, DHTML *abbrs*: dynamic hypertext markup language, a development of basic HTML code that enables you to add such features as basic animations and highlighted buttons to Web pages without relying on browser "plug-ins."

e-commerce Commercial transactions that are conducted over a network or the Internet.

e-mail *abbr.*: electronic mail, messages sent from your computer to someone else with a computer either locally through a network, or using a modem to transmit over telephone lines, usually via a central computer ("server") that stores messages in the recipient's "mailbox" until they are collected.

export A feature provided by many applications allowing you to save a file in an appropriate format so that it can be used by another application or in a different operating system. For example, an illustration created in a drawing application may be exported as an EPS file so that it can be used in a page-layout application.

file A collection of data that is stored as an individual item on a disk. A file can be a document, a folder, an application, or a resource.

file compression A technique of consolidating data within a file so that it occupies less space on a disk and is faster to transmit over telecommunications lines.

file extension The abbreviated suffix at the end of a filename that describes either its type (such as EPS or JPG) or origin (the application that created it, such as QXP for QuarkXPress files). A file extension usually comprises three letters (although Macintosh and UNIX systems may use more) and is separated from the filename by a period.

file format The way a program arranges data so that it can be stored or displayed on a computer. This can range from the file format used uniquely by a particular application, to those that are used by many different software programs. In order to help you work on a job that requires the use of several applications, or to work with other people who may be using different applications to yours, file formats tend to be standardized. Common file formats are TIFF and JPEG for bitmapped image files, EPS for object-oriented image files, and ASCII for text files.

Flash (Macromedia) Software for creating vector graphics and animations for Web presentations. Flash generates small files that are correspondingly quick to download and, being vector, are scaleable to any dimension without an increase in file size.

floating palette A palette that is available all the time and can be positioned anywhere on your screen by dragging its title bar.

folder A pictorial representation of a directory, which is the place provided by computer operating systems in which users can organize their documents, applications, and other folders (when one folder is inside another, it is said to be "nested"). Folders form the basis of the organizational system for all the data on a computer.

form A term describing fillable spaces (fields) on a Web page that provide a means of collecting information and receiving feedback from people who visit a Web site. They can be used, for example, to buy an item, answer a questionnaire, or access a database.

frame (1) An individual still image extracted from an animation sequence.

frame (2) A means of displaying more than one page at a time within a single window—the window is divided into separate areas ("frames"), each displaying a page. Although a window displaying frames may contain several pages, it is nevertheless described as a singular page. A common use of frames is to display a menu that remains static while other parts of the Web page—displayed in the same window—contain information that can, for example, be "scrolled."

gamma The measure of contrast in a digital image, implying a gradual correction of the shadow, midtone, and highlight to improve its appearance on-screen in accordance with the white point, tube type, and general calibration of the monitor. A gamma is therefore a type of color curve. An uncorrected gamma curve is said to have a value of 1.0, but can usually be varied between 0.1 and 2.9. The standard gamma setting under the Mac OS is 1.8; under Windows it is 2.2.

GIF *acronym*: graphic interchange format, a bitmapped graphics format that was originally devised by Compuserve, an Internet service provider (ISP: Compuserve is now part of AOL). The format is thus sometimes (although rarely) referred to as the "Compuserve GIF." There are two specifications, GIF87a and, more recently, GIF89a, the latter providing additional features such as transparent backgrounds. The GIF format uses a "lossless" compression technique, or "algorithm," and thus does not squeeze files as much as does the JPEG format, which is "lossy" (some data is discarded). For use in Web browsers, JPEG is the format of choice for tone images such as photographs, whereas GIF is more suitable for line images and other graphics such as text.

GIF89a see *TRANSPARENT GIF*

gradient The gradual change between two or more colors to produce an airbrushed effect. Also known as a "fountain fill," although this latter term is no longer widely used.

graphical user interface (GUI) The concept of some computer operating systems, which allows you to interact with the computer by means of pointing at graphic symbols (icons) with a mouse rather than by typing coded commands. Also known as "WIMPs" or "pointing interface."

grayscale The rendering of an image in a range of grays from white to black. In a digital image and on a monitor, this usually means that an image is rendered with eight bits assigned to each pixel, giving a maximum of 256 levels of gray. Monochrome monitors can only display black pixels, and grays are achieved by varying the number and positioning of black pixels.

GUI (*pron.*: "gooey") *acronym*: graphical user interface (see separate entry).

handheld A computer that can literally be held in the hand. Originally, the term was established to refer to ultra-compact notebook computers but is now commonly used to mean the same thing as "palmtop."

helper application Applications that assist Web browsers in delivering or displaying information such as movie or sound files.

hierarchical structure The term describing a technique of arranging information in a graded order that establishes priorities and therefore helps users find a path that leads them to what they want. Used extensively in networking and databases.

HTML *acronym*: hypertext markup language, a text-based "page description language" (PDL) used to format documents published on the World Wide Web and that can be viewed with Web browsers.

http *acronym*: hypertext transfer protocol, a text-based set of rules by which files on the World Wide Web are transferred, defining the commands that Web browsers use to communicate with Web servers. The vast majority of World Wide Web addresses, or "URLs," are prefixed with "http://."

hyperlink A contraction of "hypertext link," an embedded link to other documents, which is usually identified by being underlined or highlighted in a different color. Clicking on or selecting a hyperlink takes you to another document, part of a document, or Web site.

hypertext A programming concept that links any single word or group of words to an unlimited number of others, typically text on a Web page that has an embedded link to other documents or Web sites. Hypertext links are usually underlined and/or in a different color from the rest of the text and are activated by clicking on them.

ICC *acronym*: International Color Consortium. The organization that is responsible for defining cross-application color standards.

ICC profile see *COLOR MANAGEMENT MODULE*

ICM *acronym*: Image Color Management, the color management module incorporated into Microsoft Windows to handle ICC profiles. It is the equivalent of Apple's ColorSync.

icon In a computer's graphical user interface (GUI), this is a graphic representation of an object, such as a disk or file, or a concept or message.

image-editing application, image editor A computer application used to manipulate images that are either scanned or user-generated. Image-editing applications are pixel-based ("bitmapped" as opposed to "vector"), and provide features for preparing images for process color printing (such as color separations), as well as tools for painting and "filters" for applying special effects. Also called "image-manipulation program" or "paint program."

image map An image that contains a series of embedded links to other documents or Web sites. These links are activated when clicked on in the appropriate area of the image. For example, an image of a globe may incorporate an embedded link for each visible country that, when clicked, will take the user to a document giving more information about that country.

indexed color In some applications such as Adobe Photoshop, an image "mode" of a maximum of 256 colors that is used to reduce the file size of "RGB" images so that they can be used, for example, in multimedia presentations or Web pages. This is achieved by using an indexed table of colors ("a color look-up table," or "CLUT")—either an existing table using a known palette of "safe" colors or one constructed from an image—to which the colors in an image are matched, and, if a color in the image does not appear in the table, the application selects the nearest color or simulates it by arranging the available colors in a pattern called "dithering."

inkjet printer A printing device that creates an image by spraying tiny jets of ink onto a paper surface at high speed.

interface The physical relationship between human beings, systems, and machines—in other words, the point of interaction or connection. The involvement of humans is called a "human interface" or "user interface."

Internet The entire collection of connected worldwide networks, including those used solely for the Web. The Internet was originally funded by the U.S. Defense Department.

ISP *acronym*: Internet service provider, a term used to describe and organization that provides access to the Internet for users. At its most basic, this may be merely a telephone number for connection, but most ISPs also provide e-mail addresses and capacity for your own Web pages.

Java A programming language that was devised for the creation of small applications (applets) that can be downloaded from a Web server and used, typically in conjunction with a Web browser, to add dynamic effects such as animations.

JavaScript A "scripting" language that provides a simplified method of applying dynamic effects to Web pages.

JPEG *acronym*: Joint Photographic Experts Group, *pron.*: jay-peg. A file format for compressing bitmapped images. The degree of compression (from high compression/low-quality to low compression/ high-quality) can be defined by the user, which makes the format doubly suitable for images that are to be used either for print reproduction or for transmitting over the Internet—for viewing in Web browsers, for example.

jump list A generic springboard to other programs, sites, documents, and so on. A collection of Web links such as Bookmarks or Favorites can be a jump list, but any program can include its own jump list to take the viewer anywhere within or without the interface.

kbps *acronym*: kilobits per second, a measurement of the speed at which data is transferred across a network, a kilobit being 1,024 bits or characters.

key frame A single animation frame in a QuickTime sequence in which information is stored as a reference so that subsequent frames only store changes in the frame (differences), rather than storing the whole frame each time, thus making the file smaller.

The frames based on changes are called "delta frames" or "difference frames."

keyline The mode used by Macromedia in Freehand to describe basic shape-outline editing without colors or texture previews.

kiosk/booths A single-application computer, typically built into a rugged, secure housing and located in public places. Examples of booths include business card printing machines, public Internet access payphones, camera film developing units, and point-of-sale promotional devices. A presentation program or multimedia title that runs by itself or semi-automatically while blocking out the desktop and all other programs is said to be running in "booth mode."

layer In some applications and Web pages, a level to which you can consign an element of the design you are working on. Selected layers may be active (meaning you can work on them) or inactive. Some applications may lay items one on top of another in the order that you created them, and in some cases will let you send items to the back or bring them to the front.

LCD *acronym*: liquid crystal display. A flat-screen technology for computer monitors. LCD screens are commonly found in small devices such as wristwatches, mobile phones, handheld consoles, and palmtops, as well as a replacement for desktop CRT monitors.

link A pointer, such as a highlighted piece of text, in an HTML document (a Web page, for example) or multimedia presentation that takes the user to another location, page, or screen just by clicking on it.

Mac OS The operating system software that runs on Apple's Macintosh computer platform.

markup The technique of embedding "tags" (HTML instructions) within special characters (metacharacters) that tell a program such as a Web browser how to display a page.

markup language A defined set of rules for describing the way files are displayed by any particular method. HTML is one such language, used for creating Web pages.

marquee In some applications, this is a moving broken line drawn around an object or area

in order to "select" it or, in some cases, an area defined by an application to show that the space within is active or selected. The moving lines are colloquially known as "marching ants."

mask Any material used to protect all or part of an image or page in photomechanical reproduction, photography, illustration, or layout. Many computer applications provide a masking feature that enables you to apply a mask to all or selected parts of an image. Such masks are stored in an "alpha channel" and simulate the physical material used in platemaking that is used to shield parts of a plate from light.

masking To block out an area of an image with opaque material to prevent reproduction or to allow for modifications such as adjusting the values of color and tone.

menu The display on a computer screen showing the list of choices available to a user.

menu bar The horizontal panel across the top of a computer screen containing the titles of available menus.

menu command A command that is given to your computer from a list of choices that are available within a menu. This is distinct from a command that is made via the keyboard (keyboard command).

menu-driven A computer or application interface in which commands are given through a list of choices available from a hierarchy of menus. Synonymous with a "command-line interface."

mouse The small, handheld, mechanical device that you manipulate to position the pointer on your monitor.

mouse-event The action (event) initiated by pressing the button on your mouse. This can happen at the moment you press the button down (mouse-down) or when you release it (mouse-up).

movie The generic term that is given to any digital animation or multimedia file as well as video sequence.

MP3 *abbr.*: MPEG Audio Layer 3, a compressed audio file format. It compresses audio data by

185

shaving off the frequencies in the recording that lie beyond the range of human hearing, 20Hz to 20KHz. Further compression can be achieved by shaving off more frequency information toward the 2 to 4KHz range, within which hearing is most sensitive.

MPEG *acronym:* Motion Picture Experts Group. A compression format for squeezing full-screen, VHS-quality digital video files and animations, providing huge compression ratios of up to 200:1.

MSNBC The brand name of a Web portal site run by the U.S. television company NBC and delivered by Microsoft's on-line service MSN (Microsoft Network).

multimedia A generic term that is used for any combination of various digital media, such as sound, video, animation, graphics, and text, incorporated into a software product or presentation.

navigate The process of finding your way around a multimedia presentation or Web site by clicking on words or buttons.

navigation bar A special bar in a Web browser, Web page, or multimedia presentation that helps you to "navigate" through pages by clicking on buttons or text.

navigation button A button in a Web browser, page, or multimedia presentation that links you to a particular location or page.

nested folder In GUIs, a folder that is placed inside another folder.

on-line Any activity taking place on a computer or device while it is connected to a network such as the Internet. The opposite of off-line.

operating system The software (and in some cases "firmware") that provides the environment within which all other software and its user operates. The major operating systems are Microsoft's DOS and Windows, Apple's Mac OS, and AT&T's UNIX, the latter three of which all use GUIs.

page An HTML document (text structured with HTML tags) that is viewed with the aid of a Web browser.

page-layout/make-up application Any application that enables you to carry out all of the functions normally associated with page design, layout, and make-up.

paint(ing) application Applications that use bitmaps of pixels to create images, rather than employing the "vectors" that describe lines in drawing applications (called "object-oriented"), although some applications make use of both.

palette A window, often "floating" (movable), that contains features such as tools, measurements, or other functions.

palmtop A miniature computer, typically with LCD screen, that can be held in one hand. Some palmtops incorporate tiny keyboards, but most are operated using a stylus and touchscreen.

pane A clearly demarcated section of an on-screen window—for example, to show a document preview separately from a file listing. Similar to the concept of frames in a Web browser.

panorama A wide-angle photographic scene that can be panned and zoomed within a window, producing the illusion of natural perspective changes as the viewpoint changes.

pixel *abbr.:* picture element. The smallest component of a digitally generated image, such as a single dot of light on a computer monitor. In its simplest form, one pixel corresponds to a single bit: 0 = off, or white, and 1 = on, or black. In color or grayscale images or monitors, one pixel may correspond to several bits: an 8-bit pixel, for example, can be displayed in any of 256 colors (the total number of different configurations that can be achieved by eight 0s and 1s).

player Any software utility or plug-in that plays audio, video, or multimedia files, or even presentations.

plug-in A piece of software, usually developed by a third party, that extends the capabilities of a particular program. Plug-ins are common in image-editing and page layout applications for such things as special effect filters. Plug-ins are also common in Web browsers for such things as playing movies and audio, although these often come as complete applications (helper applications) that can be used with a number of browsers rather than any specific one.

PNG *acronym:* portable network graphics. A file format for images used on the Web that provides 10–30 percent "lossless" compression, and supports variable transparency through "alpha channels," cross-platform control of image brightness, and interlacing.

PocketPC Microsoft's Windows-compatible operating system for palmtop computers.

pointer A general term that refers to any of the many shapes on a monitor that indicate the location and operating mode of the "mouse." Typical pointer shapes are the arrow pointer, vertical bar, I-beam, crossbar or crosshair, and wristwatch. Sometimes confused with the "cursor" (the typing location within a field or piece of text).

pop-up menu A menu in a dialogue box or palette that "pops up" when you click on it. Pop-up menus usually appear as a rectangle with a drop shadow and a downward or side-pointing arrow.

portal A Web site designed to act as a computer user's doorway onto the Internet. Portal sites are filled with categorized jump lists, media services such as news and financial information, and usually access to a search engine, too.

preferences A facility provided by most applications for modifying the default program settings (such as the unit of measurement). Modifications can often be applied to a single document or, sometimes, all documents.

progressive JPEG A digital image format used for displaying JPEG images on Web pages. The image is displayed in progressively increasing resolutions as the data is downloaded to the browser. Also called "proJPEG."

QuickTime Apple's software program and system extension that enables computers running either Windows or the Mac OS to play movie and sound files, particularly over the Internet and in multimedia applications, providing cut, copy, and paste features for moving images and automatic compression and decompression of image files.

QuickTimeVR *abbr.*: QuickTime virtual reality. An Apple extension that provides features for the creation and playback of 3-D objects or panoramic scenes.

Real Media The umbrella term for Real Networks' multimedia technologies, which include Real Audio and Real Video. Real Media is highly compressed for optimum playback performance across the Internet.

RGB *acronym*: red, green, blue. The primary colors of the "additive" color model.

ribbon bar A tool bar that runs across the top of a program interface—usually just under the menu bar—which presents commonly used commands and functions (File Open, Copy, Paste, Undo, and so on) as a row of clickable buttons.

rollover The rapid substitution of one or more images when the mouse pointer is rolled over the original image. Used extensively for navigation buttons on Web pages and multimedia presentations.

RTF *acronym*: rich text format. This is an old Microsoft file format that is commonly used for cross-platform and program-independent word processing files. It contains only basic information regarding fonts, type sizes, tabs, and colors.

runtime player A small and usually free utility that lets a user view or play back a document without needing to install the original program that was used to create the document. For example, Microsoft PowerPoint includes a runtime player that you can send, along with your presentations, to people who don't have PowerPoint themselves. (QuickTime Player isn't a runtime player because it plays multimedia files regardless of which program was used to create them.)

screenful Everything that is displayed or viewable on a screen at any one moment.

scroll The action of moving an electronic document around within its on-screen window. Scrolling is normally achieved by clicking or dragging on intuitive scroll bars down the right-hand side and bottom edges of a window, but some programs allow scrolling by dragging within the document area.

selection marquee/rectangle/box A dotted line that forms a rectangle or box. The line is drawn by means of the pointer or a selection tool, and vanishes immediately after the selection is made or becomes a marquee.

search engine The part of a program such as a database that seeks out information in response to requests made by you. On the Web, search engines such as Yahoo, HotBot, and Alta Vista provide sophisticated criteria for searching, and provide summaries of each result as well as the Web site addresses for retrieving more information.

server A networked computer that serves client computers, providing a central location for files and services, and typically handling such things as e-mail and Web access.

ShockWave A technology developed by Macromedia for creating Director presentations, which can be delivered across the Internet and viewed with a Web browser.

skin A graphical overlay that changes the appearance and character of a program, but without changing its functionality.

slide show The computerized equivalent of presenting a sequence of individual projection slides onto a screen in a specific order.

SMS *acronym*: Short Messaging Service. A "store-and-forward" system of exchanging 160-character text messages between mobile phones via an SMS center.

streaming video/audio A method of transmitting video or audio that allows it to be played continuously and apparently in real time. Segments of the received data are buffered while the user's video/audio software plays the previously buffered section.

sub-menu Secondary menus that drop down or pop up from an item in a primary menu.

SWF The filetype suffix for Flash movies.

table In a Web page, the arrangement of information in "cells" that are organized in rows and columns, similar to a spreadsheet.

tag The formal name for a markup language formatting command, a tag is switched on by placing a command inside angle brackets "< >" and switched off again by repeating the same thing but additionally inserting a forward slash before the command. For example, "<bold>" makes text that follows appear in bold and "</bold>" switches bold text off.

throughput The amount of digital information processed or transmitted within a time period, often given in bits per second (bps) or kilobits per second (Kbps or Kbit/sec).

thumbnail A small on-screen preview of what a document or a page in that document looks like, allowing you to locate what you're looking for without having to open everything up laboriously one by one.

TIFF, TIF *acronym*: tagged image file format. A standard and popular graphics file format originally developed by Aldus (now merged with Adobe) and Microsoft, used for scanned, high-resolution, bitmapped images, and for color separations. The TIFF format can be used for black-and-white, grayscale, and color images that have been generated on different computer platforms.

tile, tiling The term used for repeating a graphic item and placing the repetitions side-by-side in all directions so that they form a pattern—just like tiles.

tool A feature of most graphics applications, the piece of a kit with which you perform specific tasks. A tool is a function represented by an icon that, when selected, is then used to perform the designated task, i.e., you use a box tool for creating boxes.

tool bar A fixed or floating window in a program interface that contains editing mode buttons (select, draw, paint, text, and so on).

touchscreen A computer screen that responds to touch, thereby substituting the conventional mouse. Large touchscreens are operated with a finger, while small versions are usually navigated with a round-nibbed plastic pen or "stylus."

trackball The principal alternative to a mouse as a pointing device, effectively using the old mouse-ball technology but turned upside down: instead of moving the device around to make the ball roll underneath, you keep the device stationary and manipulate the ball on top with your fingers.

187

188

transition A visual effect that is used to blend two or more frames of an animation, movie, or video.

transparent background see **TRANSPARENT GIF**

transparent GIF A feature of the graphic interchange format (see separate entry) file format that allows the user to place a non-rectangular image on top of the background color of a Web page.

trigger (or launcher) A link or button in an interface that, when activated, launches another program, opens an alternative document, or plays back a multimedia file, as opposed to simply navigating within the active interface.

tweening The automatic process of inserting additional intermediate animation frames between two existing frames (which are typically known as "key frames").

TXT Suffix used on PCs, attached to plain text files such as ASCII or ANSI files.

upload To send data from your computer to a distant computer such as a server. The opposite of download.

URL *acronym*: uniform resource locator. This is the unique address of any page on the Web, and is composed of three elements: the protocol to be used (such as http), the domain name (or "host"), and the directory name followed by pathnames to any particular file.

utility (program) A program that enhances or supports the way in which a person uses their computer generally, as distinct from those programs which enable the user to do specific work (which are known as applications). Typical utilities are programs used for backup, font management, file-finding, disk management, file recovery, plug-ins, screen savers, and so on.

viewer In this book, a viewer is a person who sees and uses your interface. Because computers tend to to work by engaging people in personal, one-to-one interaction, it would be missing the point to target an amorphous "audience." And since your interface may be accessed by non-technical people, including those who don't own or use a computer of their own, it's inaccurate to describe them as "users."

Visual Basic Microsoft's PC-only programming system for programmers who prefer not to work entirely with pure code. Visual Basic (or VB) lets you design program windows, dialogue boxes, and so on graphically, although the actual workings behind that interface still need to be programmed, of course. A lightweight variation known as Visual Basic for Applications (VBA) makes it possible to knit together the features of two or more existing compliant programs to produce a part-bespoke integrated system.

VR *acronym*: virtual reality.

VRML *acronym*: virtual reality modeling language, an HTML-type programming language designed to create 3D scenes that are called "virtual worlds."

wallpaper A graphic that is repeated or "tiled," rather in the manner of building blocks, to fill the background of a page, window, program, or desktop.

WAP *acronym*: wireless application protocol. A development of Web standards to operate on mobile phones and small-screen wireless devices such as palmtops.

watermark The technique of applying a tiled graphic to the background of a Web page, which remains fixed, no matter what foreground materials scroll across it.

Web authoring The process of creating documents (usually in HTML or XML format) for publishing on the World Wide Web.

Web browser see **BROWSER**

Web page A published HTML document on the World Wide Web.

Web server A computer (or "host") that is dedicated to Web services.

Web site The address, the location (usually on a server), and the collection of documents and resources that are used for any interlinked set of particular Web pages.

WebTV A combination of broadcast TV and a navigable computer-style interface based on Web standards, backed by Microsoft.

window An essential part of the graphical user interface that mediates between users and programming code, a window is an area of a computer screen that displays the contents of a disk, folder, or document. A window can be resized by the user, and it may also be scrolled both vertically and horizontally if the contents shown by the window are too large to fit within it.

Windows The most globally popular PC operating system, devised by Microsoft; it uses a graphical user interface similar to that which is used by the Macintosh operating system. When special software or hardware is employed, users can run Windows on Macintosh computers. However, the Macintosh OS cannot be used on PCs that were originally designed to run Windows.

WML *acronym*: wireless markup language. A development of HTML that is used for coding and presenting text, graphics, and links over wireless networks (which are commonly employed for mobile phones) and small-screen wireless devices.

World Wide Web (WWW) The term that is used to describe the entire population of Web servers, all over the world, that are connected to the Internet. The term also describes a particular type of Internet access architecture that uses a combination of HTML and various graphic formats (such as GIF and JPEG) to publish formatted text that can be read by Web browsers. Also called "the Web" or "W3."

XML *abbr.*: extensible markup language. This is a development of Web coding that is more adaptable and portable than any current version of HTML. XML's main advantages are customizability (you can use it to create your own unique, application-specific markup language beyond the limited list of HTML tags) and intelligence (while HTML knows the difference between a paragraph of text and a picture, XML can know what the text is about and what the picture shows, index both to a database, show only specific information you want to see, and so on).

INDEX

3D 34, 96–123, 180
see also VR
interfaces 120–1
packages 22
viewers 116–17, 118
virtual worlds 118–19

A
absolute URL 180
Access 85
active hyperlink 180
ActiveX 180
Adobe
Acrobat 81, 180
Gamma 61
GoLive 55, 57, 76–7, 101, 102, 111
Illustrator 24, 25
ImageReady 55
links 82
LiveMotion 57, 106
PDF format 30, 31, 44, 69, 84, 95, 111, 139
Photoshop 58, 60, 144–5
screen mode 93
aliasing 180
alignment 180
Amazon 79
anchor 180
animated GIF 98–9, 180
animation 32–3, 35, 57, 71, 96–123, 140–1, 180
antialias/antialising 180
Apple Mac 10, 11, 68
color management 61, 62–3
ColorSync 181
icons 45
OS 11, 46, 61, 134, 185
Sherlock 2 141
Web site 79
applets 18, 180
ascenders 64, 180
ASCII 180
aspect ratio 180
attachment 180
attribute 180
authoring tool 180
AvantGo 36

B
back 36, 53, 80, 90–1
backgrounds 48–9, 58, 180
bandwidth 180
banner 180
base alignment 180
baseline 180
BBC Virtual Worlds 160–1
BBC World 140
BeHere TotalView 114–15
binary code 180
binary file 180
binary system 180
bit 180
bit depth 181
bitmapped graphics 99, 181
bitmaps 104, 181
bit rate 181
blinking text 98, 100
body 181
bold 64, 65
booths 12, 13, 86, 88, 89, 126–7
color 62
definition 185
loops 93
scrolling 26
thumbnails 46
browsers 36–7, 50, 68, 84, 86, 100–1, 181
browsing 80–1, 90
Bryce 143
BThere 174
buttons 22–3, 32, 33, 52, 66–7, 74–95
Adobe Acrobat 139
definition 181
Flash 106
JavaScript 102, 103
MTV2 176
navigation 186
byte 181

C
C++ 36, 181
CAD (computer-aided design) 22, 181
Canadarm2 On-line 158–9
cap height 181

Cartoon Network 52
cartoons 98
cell 181
character 181
child 181
clip art 181
closing the loop 90–1
color
complementary 182
consistency 56–9
depth 181
essential fields 71
gamut 61, 181
graphics 41
hyperlinks 83
indexed 184
library 181
management 60–3
management module 181
management system 181–2
picker 182
table 182
text 65, 66
ColorSync 181
columns 42, 43, 66
Compaq 130–1
complementary colors 182
compression 35, 98, 182, 183
Compton's 3D World Atlas Deluxe 78
console 182
content 182
control panel 182
copyright 102
Corel 143
Draw 106
Photo-Paint 23, 113
Cortona 116, 118, 160–1
cross-platform
color management 63
definition 182
type 68–9
CSS (cascading style sheets) 101, 181
cubic VR technology 112–13
Cult3D 116, 165
cursors 18–19, 82, 182

D
Dahl, Roald 34, 168–9
data 182
database 182
default 182
Deneba Canvas 31, 55, 99, 113
Dennis Interactive 174
descenders 64, 182
desktop 182
desktop publishing 182
DHTML (dynamic HTML) 101, 168, 183
dialogue boxes/windows 20–1, 24, 34, 70, 71, 85, 182
dial-up 182
digital 182
digital data 182
digitize 182
direct mail 137
Director 36, 108–9
Disclosure 121
dithering 183
document 183
DOS 10, 183
downloading 19, 55, 59, 183
drawing application 183
Dreamweaver 55, 83, 85, 87
drilling down 17, 183
driver 183
drop-down menus 11, 16, 104, 134, 183
dynamic HTML (DHTML) 183

E
e-books 12
e-commerce 26, 27, 53, 116, 121, 157, 164–7, 183
Electrolux Screenfridge 37
e-mail
definition 183
newsletters 136–7
Enter.net 95
Entourage 21
Ericsson 129
essential field 71
Excite 26, 83
export 183

189

F

file 16, 183
  binary 180
  compression 35, 183
  extension 183
  format 183
Fira Cosmetics 165
Flash 55, 84, 88, 104–8, 109, 111, 122, 123, 156–7, 183
  Dennis Interactive 174
  G-Shock 175
  Guinness Storehouse 172
  MTV2 176
  RoaldDahl.com 168
  Wellcome Wing 162
floating palettes 22, 24–5, 145, 183
folders 16, 17, 183
  nested 186
fonts 64, 65, 68–9
forms 71, 183
  design 20–1
Forward 53, 80, 90–1
frames 86, 90, 183–4
framesets 95
FreeHand 23, 25, 107
fridges 37
FTP sites 44

G

gamma 184
  settings 62, 63
Gamma wizard 61
Gay, Jon 104
Get2Net 127
GetSmart Visa 137
GIF (graphic image format) 54, 55, 98–9, 100, 104, 180, 184
  animated 98–9, 180
  transparent 188
GoLive 55, 57, 76–7, 101, 102, 111
Google 52
graphics 38–73, 182
  see also animation
  bitmapped 99, 181
  color 41
grayscale 58, 184

Groove Radio 170
G-Shock 175
GUI (graphical user interface) 11, 16–17, 22, 184
Guinness Storehouse 6, 172

H

handheld computers 12–13, 63, 65, 93, 130–1, 184
HandSpring Visor 15
  Deluxe 93
  Edge 131
  Prism 131
Heidelberg 171
helper applications 89, 184
hierarchical structure 184
highlights 71
How Animals Move 53
HTML (hypertext markup language) 31, 36–7, 68, 72, 80, 84, 104, 105
  animation 100–2
  blinking 98
  definition 184
  dynamic 101, 168, 183
  e-mail newsletters 136–7
  G-Shock 175
  links 82
  movies 111
  ShockWave 109
  WebTV 34
  Wellcome Wing 162
http 184
hyperlinks 82–3, 184
  active 180
hypertext 36, 184

I

iCab 50
ICC (International Color Consortium) 184
  see also color management module
  profiles 61
ICM (image color management) 184
icons 18–19, 41, 71, 184
  design 44–5

Ideo 7, 171
IfYouSki.com 112
Illustrator 24, 25
image editor 184
image map 184
iMove 114, 115
indexed color 184
inkjet printer 185
integration 86–9
interactive 3D 164–5
Interactive Human Body 79
interactive movies 114–15
interactivity 33, 34–5, 84, 108–9
interface definition 185
Internet Car Company 121
Internet definition 185
Internet Explorer 12, 19, 32, 68–9, 166
Internet radio 129
iPIX 112, 113, 167
ISP (Internet service provider) 185
italics 64

J

Java 102, 185
  applets 18, 180
JavaScript 84, 102–3, 185
  rollovers 82, 102, 103, 105
JPEG (Joint Photographics Experts Group) 54, 55, 98, 185, 186
jump list 185

K

Kai's Power Tools 142
kbps (kilobits per second) 185
key frame 185
keyline 185
Krause, Kai 142

L

language 53
launchers 84–5, 188
layers 28–9, 101, 107, 185
layout principles 42–3
LCD (liquid crystal display) 14, 54, 185
legibility 66–7

Lingo 108
links 28, 36, 52, 66–7, 74–95, 185
LiveMotion 57, 106
logical overheads 52–3
loops
  closing 90–1
  escaping 92–3
LudiWAP 132
Lycos 83

M

Macromedia
  Director 36, 108–9
  Dreamweaver 55, 83, 85, 87
  Fireworks 55
  Flash 55, 84, 88, 104–8, 109, 111, 122, 123, 156–7, 183
    Dennis Interactive 174
    G-Shock 175
    Guinness Storehouse 172
    MTV2 176
    RoaldDahl.com 168
    Wellcome Wing 162
  FreeHand 23, 25, 107
  ShockMachine 141
  ShockWave 18, 105, 108–9, 111, 123, 141, 187
Man Roland 164
markup 185
markup language 185
  see also HTML; XML
marquee 185
mask 185
masking 185
Media Player 51, 88, 110, 150–1
menu 185
menu bar 185
menu command 185
menu-driven 185
messages 20–1
MetaCreations 142
  Bryce 143
Microsoft
  Access 85
  ActiveX 180
  Entourage 21
  Internet Explorer 12, 19, 32, 68–9, 166

Office 22, 23, 46, 47
PocketPC 12, 69, 131, 186
Publisher 56
Visual Basic 188
Windows 10
  color management 61, 62–3
  cursors 18
  definition 188
  Media Player 51, 88, 110,
    150–1
  themes 51
  thumbnails 46
  VBA 84
  XP 10, 91, 135
Word 21, 22, 23, 25, 89
mobile phones 14–15, 27, 37, 86,
  132–3
  future 128
  loops 92–3
  overheads 52, 54
  voice-operated dialling 78
modem speed 55
Montréal en Lumère 156
mouse 185
mouse event 185
movies 87, 110–11, 140, 186
  see also animation
  interactive 114–15
MP3 audio 44, 50, 88, 146, 186
mp3.com 136
MPEG (Motion Picture Experts
  Group) 186
MSNBC 43, 186
MTV2 176–7
multimedia 32–3, 34, 53, 78, 84,
  8, 109, 140–1, 186
multiple platforms 12–15
multiple programs 88–9
multiple windows 86–7
MusicMatch 136–7
  Jukebox 148–9

N
navigation 7, 30–1, 49, 76–95,
  172–3, 186
  Adobe Acrobat 139
  bar 186
  button 186

color 56
  typography 65
nested folders 186
Netscape 50, 69
  Composer 32
New Museum of Contemporary
  Art 81
newsletters 136–7
Nike 166
Nokia 128
Norton Utilities 45

O
Office 22, 23, 46, 47
Onboard 136
on-line 186
Openwave 133
operating systems 186
"Oscar the Balloonist" 78
overheads
  logical 52–3
  technical 54–5
overlays 50–1

P
Padova, Ted 139
page 186
  layout 186
Paintbrush cursor 18
painting application 186
Paint Shop Pro 20, 23
palettes 186
  floating 22, 24–5, 145, 183
palmtops 12, 15, 36–7, 71, 128,
  130–1
  color 63
  definition 186
  fonts 69
  text size 67
  ·Web explosion 36–7
pane 186
panoramas 112–13, 114–15, 123,
  167, 186
Parallel Graphics 164
  Cortona 116, 118, 160–1
  Internet Character Animator
    119
  Internet Scene Assembler 119

photographs 58
Photo-Paint 23, 113
Photoshop 58, 60, 144–5
pixel 186
playback movies 110–11
player 186
plug-in 186
PNG (portable network graphic)
  54, 55, 186
PocketPC 12, 69, 131, 186
pointer 186
point-of-sale booths
  see booths
pop-ups 70, 71, 82, 84, 114, 186
portal 186
PowerPoint 30–1, 35, 55, 57,
  80–1, 88, 89, 92–3
  GIF 98
  movies 111
  ShockWave 109
preferences 186
printers 185
progressive browsing 80–1, 90
progressive JPEG 186
progressive paging 28–9
Publisher 56
Pulse 3D 116, 117
PuppetTime 119

Q
Quark XPress 21
Quicken Deluxe 33
QuickTime 31, 44, 88, 110–11,
  140, 186–7
QuickTime VR (Virtual Reality)
  112–13, 121, 123, 162, 187

R
radio 129
Real Media 187
Real Player 88
RealPool 109
RealVideo format 111
RGB 187
ribbon bars 22–3, 32, 187
Rosen, Avi 121
RTF 187
runtime player 36, 187

S
Science Museum Wellcome Wing
  120, 162–3
Screenfridge 37
screenful 187
screensavers 133
scrolling 11, 26–7, 43, 170, 187
scrolling marquee 100–1
search engine 187
selection marquee 187
server 187
ShockMachine 141
ShockWave 18, 105, 108–9, 111,
  123, 141, 187
signposting 78–9
silk-screen areas 131
skins 7, 50–1, 146–55, 187
Sky Digital 138
slide shows 30–1, 187
slide transitions 35
SmoothMove's iMove 114, 115
SMS (Short Messaging Service)
  187
Sonique 152–5
sound 32–3, 78
space saving 144–5
spam 137
spherical video 114, 115
splash screen 94
streaming video/audio 187
sub-menu 187
Surf Europe 136
SWF 106, 107, 187

T
table 187
tag 187
TAGHeuer 137
technical overheads 54–5
Techsys 157
throughput 187
thumbnails 7, 46–7, 71, 89, 171,
  187
TIFF 54, 55, 187
tile 187
tool 187
tool bars 22–3, 187
TotalView 114–15

touch screen 187
trackball 187–8
transition 188
transparent GIF 188
triggers 84–5, 102, 103, 109, 188
tweening 188
TXT 188
type 41
typography 64–9

U
upload 188
URL (Uniform Resource Locator)
    90, 188
    absolute 180
utility program 188

V
Vans 126
VBA (Visual Basis for
    Applications) 84
vector animation 57, 99, 104–7
viewer 188
ViewPoint 116
Virtual Air Sites 167
virtual tour 120
virtual worlds 118–19
Visual Basic 188
visual signposting 78–9
voice-operated programs 78
VR (Virtual Reality) technology
    112–23, 156–67, 188
VRML (virtual reality modelling
    language) 116, 118–19, 120,
    188
    BBC Virtual Worlds 160–1
    Man Roland 164
    Science Museum Wellcome
        Wing 162–3
VR Toolbox, VR Panoworx 113

W
wallpaper 48, 50, 58, 133, 188
WAP (wireless application
    protocol) 86, 132–3, 188
    browsers 92–3
    LudiWAP 132
    sites 14–15, 27, 37, 52, 54

watermark 188
Web authoring 188
Webbackground.com 48
Web browser see browser
Web explosion 7, 36–7, 80
Web page 188
Web Screen H610 129
Web server 188
Web site 188
WebTV 34, 188
WinAmp 146–7
Windows see Microsoft, Windows
windows 188
    dialogue 20–1, 24, 34, 70, 71,
    85,
        182
    multiple 86–7
WinZip 35
Wizard mode 35
WML (wireless markup language)
    188
Word 21, 22, 23, 25, 89
WWW (World Wide Web) 188

X
XML (Extensible Markup
    Language) 109, 188

Y
Yahoo 43, 70, 83

Z
Z-Write 21